Technical and Bibliographic Notes/Notes techniques et bibliographiques

The Institute has attempted to obtain the best original copy available for filming. Features of this copy which may be bibliographically unique, which may alter any of the images in the reproduction, or which may significantly change the usual method of filming, are checked below.

L'Institut a microfilmé le meilleur exemplaire qu'il lui a été possible de se procurer. Les détails de cet exemplaire qui sont peut-être uniques du point de vue bibliographique, qui peuvent modifier une image reproduite, ou qui peuvent exiger une modification dans la méthode normale de filmage sont indiqués ci-dessous.

- [ ] Coloured covers/ Couverture de couleur
- [ ] Covers damaged/ Couverture endommagée
- [ ] Covers restored and/or laminated/ Couverture restaurée et/ou pelliculée
- [ ] Cover title missing/ Le titre de couverture manque
- [ ] Coloured maps/ Cartes géographiques en couleur
- [ ] Coloured ink (i.e. other than blue or black)/ Encre de couleur (i.e. autre que bleue ou noire)
- [x] Coloured plates and/or illustrations/ Planches et/ou illustrations en couleur
- [ ] Bound with other material/ Relié avec d'autres documents
- [ ] Tight binding may cause shadows or distortion along interior margin/ La reliure serrée peut causer de l'ombre ou de la distortion le long de la marge intérieure
- [ ] Blank leaves added during restoration may appear within the text. Whenever possible, these have been omitted from filming/ Il se peut que certaines pages blanches ajoutées lors d'une restauration apparaissent dans le texte, mais, lorsque cela était possible, ces pages n'ont pas été filmées.
- [ ] Coloured pages/ Pages de couleur
- [ ] Pages damaged/ Pages endommagées
- [ ] Pages restored and/or laminated/ Pages restaurées et/ou pelliculées
- [x] Pages discoloured, stained or foxed/ Pages décolorées, tachetées ou piquées
- [ ] Pages detached/ Pages détachées
- [x] Showthrough/ Transparence
- [ ] Quality of print varies/ Qualité inégale de l'impression
- [ ] Includes supplementary material/ Comprend du matériel supplémentaire
- [ ] Only edition available/ Seule édition disponible
- [ ] Pages wholly or partially obscured by errata slips, tissues, etc., have been refilmed to ensure the best possible image/ Les pages totalement ou partiellement obscurcies par un feuillet d'errata, une pelure, etc., ont été filmées à nouveau de façon à obtenir la meilleure image possible.
- [x] Additional comments:/ Commentaires supplémentaires: Irregular pagination : [i] - viii, [i] - viii, [1] - [108] p.

This item is filmed at the reduction ratio checked below/
Ce document est filmé au taux de réduction indiqué ci-dessous.

10X		12X		14X		16X		18X		20X		22X		24X		26X		28X		30X		32X
											✓											

The copy filmed here has been reproduced thanks to the generosity of:

National Library of Canada

The images appearing here are the best quality possible considering the condition and legibility of the original copy and in keeping with the filming contract specifications.

Original copies in printed paper covers are filmed beginning with the front cover and ending on the last page with a printed or illustrated impression, or the back cover when appropriate. All other original copies are filmed beginning on the first page with a printed or illustrated impression, and ending on the last page with a printed or illustrated impression.

The last recorded frame on each microfiche shall contain the symbol —► (meaning "CONTINUED"), or the symbol ▼ (meaning "END"), whichever applies.

Maps, plates, charts, etc., may be filmed at different reduction ratios. Those too large to be entirely included in one exposure are filmed beginning in the upper left hand corner, left to right and top to bottom, as many frames as required. The following diagrams illustrate the method:

L'exemplaire filmé fut reproduit grâce à la générosité de:

Bibliothèque nationale du Canada

Les images suivantes ont été reproduites avec le plus grand soin, compte tenu de la condition et de la netteté de l'exemplaire filmé, et en conformité avec les conditions du contrat de filmage.

Les exemplaires originaux dont la couverture en papier est imprimée sont filmés en commençant par le premier plat et en terminant soit par la dernière page qui comporte une empreinte d'impression ou d'illustration, soit par le second plat, selon le cas. Tous les autres exemplaires originaux sont filmés en commençant par la première page qui comporte une empreinte d'impression ou d'illustration et en terminant par la dernière page qui comporte une telle empreinte.

Un des symboles suivants apparaîtra sur la dernière image de chaque microfiche, selon le cas: le symbole —► signifie "A SUIVRE", le symbole ▼ signifie "FIN".

Les cartes, planches, tableaux, etc., peuvent être filmés à des taux de réduction différents. Lorsque le document est trop grand pour être reproduit en un seul cliché, il est filmé à partir de l'angle supérieur gauche, de gauche à droite, et de haut en bas, en prenant le nombre d'images nécessaire. Les diagrammes suivants illustrent la méthode.

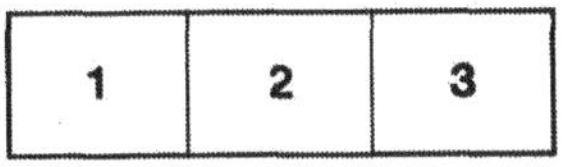

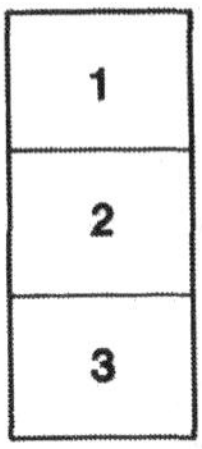

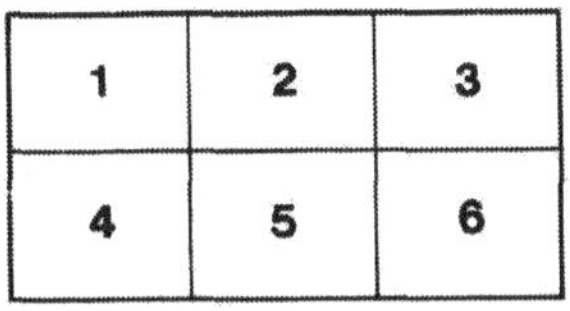

BY CO

BY COMMAND OF His late Majesty WILLIAM THE IVTH

and under the Patronage of

Her Majesty the Queen.

HISTORICAL RECORDS,

OF THE

British Army

Comprising the

History of every Regiment

IN HER MAJESTY'S SERVICE.

By Richard Cannon Esqre

Adjutant General's Office, Horse Guards.

London.

Printed by Authority:

(1837.)

HISTORICAL RECORDS

OF

THE BRITISH ARMY.

GENERAL ORDERS.

HORSE-GUARDS,
1st January, 1836.

His Majesty has been pleased to command, that, with a view of doing the fullest justice to Regiments, as well as to Individuals who have distinguished themselves by their Bravery in Action with the Enemy, an Account of the Services of every Regiment in the British Army shall be published under the superintendence and direction of the Adjutant-General; and that this Account shall contain the following particulars, viz.,

—— The Period and Circumstances of the Original Formation of the Regiment; The Stations at which it has been from time to time employed; The Battles, Sieges, and other Military Operations, in which it has been engaged, particularly specifying any Achievement it may have performed, and the Colours, Trophies, &c., it may have captured from the Enemy.

—— The Names of the Officers and the number of Non-Commissioned Officers and Privates, Killed or Wounded by the Enemy, specifying the Place and Date of the Action.

—— The Names of those Officers, who, in consideration of their Gallant Services and Meritorious Conduct in Engagements with the Enemy, have been distinguished with Titles, Medals, or other Marks of His Majesty's gracious favour.

—— The Names of all such Officers, Non-Commissioned Officers and Privates as may have specially signalized themselves in Action.

And,

—— The Badges and Devices which the Regiment may have been permitted to bear, and the Causes on account of which such Badges or Devices, or any other Marks of Distinction, have been granted.

By Command of the Right Honourable

GENERAL LORD HILL,
Commanding-in-Chief.

JOHN MACDONALD,
Adjutant-General.

PREFACE.

The character and credit of the British Army must chiefly depend upon the zeal and ardour, by which all who enter into its service are animated, and consequently it is of the highest importance that any measure calculated to excite the spirit of emulation, by which alone great and gallant actions are achieved, should be adopted.

Nothing can more fully tend to the accomplishment of this desirable object, than a full display of the noble deeds with which the Military History of our country abounds. To hold forth these bright examples to the imitation of the youthful soldier, and thus to incite him to emulate the meritorious conduct of those who have preceded him in their honourable career, are among the motives that have given rise to the present publication.

The operations of the British Troops are, indeed, announced in the "London Gazette," from whence they are transferred into the public prints: the achievements of our armies are thus made known at the time of their occurrence, and receive the tribute of praise and admiration to which they are entitled. On extraordinary occasions, the Houses of Parliament have been in the habit of conferring on the Commanders, and the Officers and Troops acting under their orders, expressions of approbation and of thanks for their skill and bravery, and these testimonials, confirmed by the high honour of their Sovereign's Approbation, constitute the reward which the soldier most highly prizes.

It has not, however, until late years, been the practice (which appears to have long prevailed in some of the Continental armies) for British Regiments to keep regular records of their services and achievements. Hence some difficulty has been experienced in obtaining, particularly from the old Regiments, an authentic account of their origin and subsequent services.

This defect will now be remedied, in consequence of His Majesty having been pleased to command, that every Regiment shall in future keep a full and ample record of its services at home and abroad.

From the materials thus collected, the country will henceforth derive information as to the difficulties and privations which chequer the career of those who embrace the military profession. In Great Britain, where so large a number of persons are devoted to the active concerns of agriculture, manufactures, and commerce, and where these pursuits have, for so long a period, been undisturbed by the *presence of war*, which few other countries have escaped, comparatively little is known of the vicissitudes of active service, and of the casualties of climate, to which, even during peace, the British Troops are exposed in every part of the globe, with little or no interval of repose.

In their tranquil enjoyment of the blessings which the

country derives from the industry and the enterprise of the agriculturist and the trader, its happy inhabitants may be supposed not often to reflect on the perilous duties of the soldier and the sailor,—on their sufferings,—and on the sacrifice of valuable life, by which so many national benefits are obtained and preserved.

The conduct of the British Troops, their valour, and endurance, have shone conspicuously under great and trying difficulties; and their character has been established in Continental warfare by the irresistible spirit with which they have effected debarkations in spite of the most formidable opposition, and by the gallantry and steadiness with which they have maintained their advantages against superior numbers.

In the official Reports made by the respective Commanders, ample justice has generally been done to the gallant exertions of the Corps employed; but the details of their services, and of acts of individual bravery, can only be fully given in the Annals of the various Regiments.

These Records are now preparing for publication, under His Majesty's special authority, by Mr. Richard Cannon, Principal Clerk of the Adjutant-General's Office; and while the perusal of them cannot fail to be useful and interesting to military men of every rank, it is considered that they will also afford entertainment and information to the general reader, particularly to those who may have served in the Army, or who have relatives in the Service.

There exists in the breasts of most of those who have

served, or are serving, in the Army, an *Esprit de Corps*—an attachment to every thing belonging to their Regiment; to such persons a narrative of the services of their own Corps cannot fail to prove interesting. Authentic accounts of the actions of the great,—the valiant,—the loyal, have alway been of paramount interest with a brave and civilized people. Great Britain has produced a race of heroes who, in moments of danger and terror, have stood, "firm as the rocks of their native shore;" and when half the World has been arrayed against them, they have fought the battles of their Country with unshaken fortitude. It is presumed that a record of achievements in war,—victories so complete and surprising, gained by our countrymen,—our brothers,—our fellow-citizens in arms,—a record which revives the memory of the brave, and brings their gallant deeds before us, will certainly prove acceptable to the public.

Biographical memoirs of the Colonels and other distinguished Officers, will be introduced in the Records of their respective Regiments, and the Honorary Distinctions which have, from time to time, been conferred upon each Regiment, as testifying the value and importance of its services, will be faithfully set forth.

As a convenient mode of Publication, the Record of each Regiment will be printed in a distinct number, so that when the whole shall be completed, the Parts may be bound up in numerical succession.

HISTORICAL RECORD

OF

THE ELEVENTH,

OR

THE PRINCE ALBERT'S OWN,

REGIMENT OF

HUSSARS:

CONTAINING AN ACCOUNT OF

THE FORMATION OF THE REGIMENT

IN 1715,

AND OF

ITS SUBSEQUENT SERVICES

TO

1842.

LONDON:
JOHN W. PARKER, WEST STRAND.

M.DCCC.XLIII.

LONDON:
HARRISON AND CO., PRINTERS,
ST. MARTIN'S LANE.

THE ELEVENTH,

OR

PRINCE ALBERT'S OWN

HUSSARS,

BEAR ON THEIR APPOINTMENTS THE

"SPHINX," WITH THE WORDS "EGYPT,"

"SALAMANCA," "PENINSULA."

"WATERLOO,"

AND

"BHURTPORE."

CONTENTS.

Year		Page
1715	Formation of the Regiment	1
——	Names of the Officers	2
——	Costume	—
——	Engaged with the Rebels at Preston	4
1722	Encamped on Hounslow Heath	5
1727	Under orders for foreign service	6
1733	Reviewed by King George II.	—
1745	Rebellion	7
1746	Proceeds to Scotland	—
——	Battle of Culloden	8
1751	Description of the standards and clothing	9
1755	A light troop added	12
1758	Expeditions to St. Maloes and Cherbourg	13
1760	Proceeds to Germany	14
——	Battle of Warbourg	15
1761	Incursion into the enemy's quarters	16
——	Battle of Kirch Denkern	—
——	Actions at Capelnhagen and Foorwohle	17
1762	Battle of Groebenstien	—
——	Covering the siege of Cassel	—
1763	Returns to England	18
——	Light Troop disbanded	—
——	Eight men per troop equipped as Light Dragoons	—
1767	Marches to Scotland	—
1768	Returns to England	—
1772	Proceeds to Scotland	—
1773	Returns to England	—

Year		Page
1778	Stationed in Scotland	19
1779	Returns to England	—
1780	Riots in London	—
1783	Constituted a Corps of *Light Dragoons*	—
1784	Uniform changed from *scarlet* to *blue*	—
1791	Riots at Birmingham	20
1792	Encamped on Bagshot Heath	21
1793	Two Squadrons embark for Flanders	—
——	Detachments to the West Indies, and to China	22
——	Action at Famars	—
——	Covering the siege of Valenciennes	23
——	———————— Dunkirk	—
1794	Action at Prémont	24
——	Covering the siege of Landrécies	—
——	Action at Villers en Couché	24
——	Battle of Cateau	25
——	—— of Tournay	26
1795	Skirmish at Geldermalsen	28
——	Retreat through Holland to Germany	—
——	Embarks for England	29
1796	Encamped near Weymouth	30
——	Alterations in the clothing	—
1798	Encamped on Swinley Downs	30
1799	Embarks for Holland	—
——	Actions at Walmenhuysen, &c.	31
——	Battle of Egmont-op-zee	—
——	Action at Beverwyck	32
——	Returns to England	33
1800	Detachment to the Mediterranean	33
——	Expedition to Egypt	—
1801	Battle of Alexandria	34
——	Action at Rahmanie	36
——	Capture of Cairo and Alexandria	—
1802	Detachment returns to England	37
1807	Embarks for Ireland	39

Year		Page
1810	Returns to England	39
1811	Proceeds to Portugal	40
——	Action on the Caya	41
——	——— at St. Martin de Trebejo	44
——	——— Pastores	—
——	——— El Bodon	45
1812	Covering the siege of Badajoz	50
——	Skirmishes near Salamanca	51
——	Action at Castrejon	52
——	Battle of Salamanca	53
——	Rencounter near La Serna	54
——	——— at Tudela	55
——	——— Casteringa	56
——	——— Torquemada	57
——	——— Monasterie	—
——	——— Cellada del Camino	58
1813	Returns to England	59
1815	Proceeds to the Netherlands	63
——	Battle of Quatre Bras	64
——	Skirmishes at Genappe	—
——	Battle of Waterloo	65
——	Advances to Paris	69
——	Forms part of the army of occupation in France	—
1816 to 1818	Reviews, &c.,—Returns to England	70
1819	Proceeds to India	71
1825	Siege of Bhurtpore	74
1830	Clothing exchanged from *blue* to *scarlet*	77
1838	Returns to England	80
1839	Reviews, &c.,—Good appearance of the Regiment	81
1840	Escorts Prince Albert of Saxe Cobourg	85
——	Equipped as *Hussars* and styled *Prince Albert's Own*	85
——	Clothing changed from *scarlet* to *blue*	86

Year		Page
1840	Address from the Citizens, &c., of Canterbury .	86
1841	Furnishes Escorts for the Queen	89
1842	———— for the King of Prussia .	91
——	Reviewed by the Queen	92
——	The Conclusion	93

SUCCESSION OF COLONELS.

1715	Philip Honeywood	95
1732	Lord Mark Kerr	97
1752	William Henry Earl of Ancram . . .	99
1775	James Johnston	100
1785	Honorable Thomas Gage	—
1787	Joseph Lord Dover, K.B.	101
1789	Studholme Hodgson	102
1798	William John Marquis of Lothian, K.T. .	103
1813	Lord William Henry Cavendish Bentinck .	104
1839	Lord Charles Somerset Manners, K.C.B. .	106
1839	Philip Philpot	—
1840	His Royal Highness Francis Albert Augustus Charles Emanuel, Duke of Saxe, Prince of Saxe Cobourg and Gotha, K.G., G.C.B. .	107
1842	Arthur Benjamin Clifton, K.C.B. . . .	107
1842	Charles Murray, Lord Greenock, K.C.B. .	107

Page
86
89
91
92
93

95
97
99
100
—
101
102
103
104
106
—

107
107
107

ELEVENTH, THE PRINCE ALBERT'S OWN, HUSSARS.

FOR CANNON'S MILITARY RECORDS

HISTORICAL RECORD

OF

THE ELEVENTH,

OR,

PRINCE ALBERT'S OWN

HUSSARS.

THE peaceful accession of King George I. to the throne of Great Britain and Ireland, on the 1st of August, 1714, appeared to extinguish the hopes of the adherents of the Stuart dynasty; and this happy event, occurring at the close of a long and sanguinary war, which had wasted the resources of the states of Europe, was hailed as a guarantee for the preservation of the Protestant religion, and as the harbinger of years of peace and prosperity. The expectations of the people were, however, only realized in part. The friends of the Pretender soon recovered from the consternation into which they had been thrown, and their exertions to kindle the flame of civil war in Great Britain, and to procure the aid of a foreign force to place the Chevalier de St. George on the throne, rendered it necessary, in the summer of 1715, for his Majesty to augment the army. 1715

1715 Brigadier-General Philip Honeywood, who had commanded a regiment of foot in the preceding reign, and who had acquired the reputation of a brave, experienced, zealous officer, firmly devoted to the interests of the house of Hanover, was selected, on this emergency, to raise and discipline a regiment of dragoons, of which he was appointed colonel; and this corps having been continued in the service of the crown to the present time, now bears the title of The Eleventh, Prince Albert's Own, Regiment of Hussars.

The warrant for raising this corps, was dated the 22nd of July, 1715; the regiment was directed to consist of six troops, to be raised in Essex and in the adjoining counties; and Chelmsford was appointed as the general rendezvous of the corps. The following officers were appointed to commissions in the regiment:—

Captains.	*Lieutenants.*	*Cornets.*
Phil. Honeywood, (Col.)	Jno. Maitland, (Capt.-Lt.)	Jno. Campbell
A. Hamilton, (Lt.-Col.)	Wm. Lemmon	Wm. Robt. Adaire
Hump. Bland, (Major)	James Maule	Chas. Wheeler
John Suckling	—— Malkin	John Burroughs
Benj. Huffam	Chas. Stewart	Wm. Gardner
Wm. Robinson	Jno. Mitchell	—— [illegible]

The uniform was three-cornered cocked hats, bound with silver lace; scarlet coats, lined and

turned up with buff; buff waistcoats and breeches, 1715
and boots of jacked leather; also buff horse-furniture: and the regiment bore on its guidons, in common with the remainder of the army, the white horse of Brunswick, the badge of the house of Hanover*.

Riots and disturbances had occurred in various parts of the country previous to the issue of the warrant for raising the regiment; and before the several troops were complete and ready for service, the Earl of Mar raised the Pretender's standard in Scotland, and assembled an army of ten thousand men. He was opposed by the King's troops, under the Duke of Argyle, and "HONEYWOOD'S DRAGOONS" (the title by which the regiment was then distinguished) were detained in England to overawe the Jacobins; and on the 19th of October the regiment received an order to march from Chelmsford to Nottingham. A small division of the rebel army penetrated into South Britain, and, being joined by a number of English insurgents, advanced into Lancashire; when HONEYWOOD'S Dragoons were called from their cantonments at Notting-

* There has long been a tradition in the regiment, that it was originally mounted on grey horses, and bore on its standards the motto, *Motus componere;* the statement is not, however, corroborated by royal warrant, or other authentic documentary evidence.

1715 ham to confront the rebel bands, which had taken possession of Preston.

On the 12th of November a regiment of horse, five of dragoons, and one of foot, commanded by Major-General Wills, approached the town of *Preston*, where the rebels had thrown up entrenchments, erected barricades, and planted cannon, to defend themselves against the royal forces. The ELEVENTH Dragoons were formed in brigade with Wynne's (now Ninth Royal Lancers), commanded by Brigadier-General Honeywood.

Having driven in the rebel piquets, preparations were made for attacking the barricades. Fifty men of the ELEVENTH Dragoons dismounted, to take part with the infantry in storming the avenue leading to Wigan, and the regiment moved forward to support the attack. The first barrier was speedily carried, and the rebels driven behind the second barricade, which could not be forced, for want of cannon. The foot and dismounted dragoons took possession of two houses, from whence they opened a sharp fire on the rebels; a breastwork was afterwards thrown across the road, and the houses between the breastwork and the barricade were set on fire: at the same time, the combat of musketry was continued until darkness stayed the work of destruction. On the following day the rebels beat a parley, and additional troops having 1715 arrived under Major-General Carpenter, they afterwards surrendered at discretion.

Brigadier-General Honeywood received a wound in the shoulder, and Major Bland a wound in the arm; the regiment had also five private soldiers and twelve horses wounded.

The regiment was subsequently quartered in 1716 Lancashire; and when the rebellion in Scotland was suppressed, in the early part of 1716, it marched into Gloucestershire and Worcestershire, but returned to Lancashire in the autumn.

In the early part of 1717 the regiment was 1717 stationed in Staffordshire; in the autumn it was removed into Lincolnshire; and in 1718 it was 1718 stationed,—three troops at Stamford and three at Peterborough: at the same time the establishment was reduced from forty to twenty-five private soldiers per troop;—the total being two hundred and seven officers and men;—and the estimated expense 11,226*l.* 15*s.* 10*d.* per annum.

In 1719 the regiment was quartered at 1719 Gloucester and Tewksbury, and subsequently at Shrewsbury, Ludlow, and Bridgenorth; in 1720 1720 and 1721 it occupied cantonments at Coventry, 1721 Warwick and Lutterworth; in the summer of 1722 it was encamped on Hounslow-heath, with 1722 the Royal Horse Guards and King's Horse, now

1722 First Dragoon Guards, and was reviewed by King George I. on the 5th of July.

1723 During the succeeding five years the esta-
1724 blishment was between three and four hundred
1725 officers and men, and the regiment was generally
1726 stationed in the southern and midland counties of England.

1727 On the prospect of Great Britain being involved in a German war, the regiment was augmented, in 1727, to five hundred and fifty-two men, and it was held in readiness to proceed abroad; but no embarkation took place; and in
1728 the spring of 1728 it marched to Scotland, where the establishment was reduced to three hundred and nine men.

1729 From Scotland, the regiment marched in
1730 1729 into Lancashire; in 1730 it was in Berk-
1731 shire; in 1731 and 1732 in Leicestershire and Staffordshire.

1732 After commanding the regiment upwards of sixteen years, Philip Honeywood was removed in May, 1732, to the Third Dragoons, and the colonelcy of the ELEVENTH was conferred by King George II. on Lord Mark Kerr, from the Thirteenth regiment of Foot.

1733 In April, 1733, the ELEVENTH marched to village cantonments, near Hounslow, and were reviewed on the 12th of May on Hounslow-heath, by King George II., who was pleased to

express his royal approbation of their appearance 1733
and discipline.

After the review the regiment returned to Staffordshire, where it was stationed in 1734; in 1734
1735 it occupied quarters at Gloucester and 1735
Hereford, and in 1736 at Norwich and Lynn. 1736

A succession of marches, similar to those 1737
already narrated, was performed by the regiment during the following eight years. On the breaking out of the war with Spain in 1739, the esta- 1739
blishment was augmented to four hundred and thirty-five men. The Emperor Charles VI. died in 1740; and this event was followed by a war 1740
between the Archduchess Maria Theresa and the Elector of Bavaria, respecting the kingdom of Bohemia. France took part with the Elector, 1741
and Great Britain with the house of Austria; and in 1742 King George II. sent an army to 1742
the Netherlands. The ELEVENTH Dragoons were detained on home service, and were stationed in England in 1745, when Charles Edward, eldest 1745
son of the Pretender, arrived in Scotland, and summoned the Highland clans to arms.

The movements of the regiment were connected with the operations of the rebels, who penetrated England as far as Derby, but afterwards made a precipitate retreat to Scotland.

In January, 1746, the ELEVENTH Dragoons 1746
were quartered on the confines of Scotland; the

1746 rebel army was besieging Stirling castle, and Lieut.-General Hawley advanced with a small force to raise the siege; but was defeated at Falkirk on the 17th of January, and returned to Edinburgh. After this disaster the regiment was ordered to march to Edinburgh, where it arrived before the end of January. The Duke of Cumberland assumed the command of the forces, and advanced against the rebels. The ELEVENTH Dragoons, commanded by Lieut.-Colonel the EARL OF ANCRAM, (afterwards Marquis of Lothian,) were in advance; but the main body of the rebel army fled with such precipitation that it could not be overtaken by the King's forces.

Following the retiring Highlanders, the regiment arrived at Aberdeen, where it was quartered for some time, the weather being too severe to continue military operations. The army was again in motion in the beginning of April; and on the 16th of that month the rebels were discovered in position on *Culloden* Moor; the royal forces formed in order of battle, and the ELEVENTH Dragoons, commanded by Lieut.-Colonel LORD ANCRAM, took post on the left of the first line. After a severe cannonade had been kept up some time, a select body of the Highlanders charged sword in hand: they were received with the bayonet; and the prowess and discipline of the King's infantry proved superior

to the irregular valour of the clans. A charge 1746
of the cavalry completed the overthrow of the rebel host; and the Highlanders were pursued with dreadful slaughter for several miles. After returning from the pursuit, the ELEVENTH Dragoons were thanked by the Duke of Cumberland for their gallant and zealous conduct. Their loss was limited to three men and four horses killed; three men and fifteen horses wounded.

The rebellion was thus finally suppressed. Attempts were made to intercept the young Pretender; and on the 30th of April, Colonel the Earl of Ancram marched with the ELEVENTH Dragoons for the eastern coast; but the Pretender, after wandering among the isles and mountains a wretched fugitive for some time, escaped to France.

The war on the continent was terminated in 1748
1748 by a treaty of peace; and in 1749 the 1749
establishment was reduced to two hundred and eighty-five men.

On the 1st of July, 1751, King George II. 1751
issued a warrant for establishing uniformity in the clothing, standards, and colours of the several regiments, from which the following particulars have been extracted respecting the

ELEVENTH DRAGOONS.

COATS, — scarlet, double-breasted, without lappels, lined with *buff;* slit sleeves, turned up

1751 with buff; the button-holes ornamented with narrow white lace; the buttons flat, of white metal, set on three and three; a slash pocket in each skirt; and a white worsted aiguillette on the right shoulder.

WAISTCOATS AND BREECHES,—buff.

HATS,—bound with silver lace, and ornamented with a black cockade and a white metal loop: the forage cap red, turned up with buff, and the rank of the regiment on the flap.

BOOTS,—of jacked leather, reaching up to the knee.

CLOAKS,—of scarlet cloth, with a buff cape, and lined with buff shalloon; the buttons set on three and three on white frogs or loops, with a green stripe down the centre.

HORSE FURNITURE,—of buff cloth; the holster caps and housings having a border of white lace, with a green stripe down the centre; XI. D. embroidered on the housings, on a red ground, within a wreath of roses and thistles; on the holster caps the King's cipher, with the crown over it, and XI. D. underneath.

OFFICERS,—distinguished by silver lace; their coats and waistcoats bound with silver embroidery; the button-holes worked with silver; and a crimson silk sash worn across the left shoulder.

QUARTER MASTERS,—to wear a crimson silk sash round their waists.

SERJEANTS,—to have narrow silver lace on their cuffs, pockets, and shoulder-straps; silver aiguillettes; and green and buff worsted sashes round their waists. 1751

CORPORALS,—narrow silver lace on the cuffs and shoulder-straps; and a white silk aiguillette.

DRUMMERS AND HAUTBOYS, — buff-coats lined with white lace, with a green stripe down the centre; red waistcoats and breeches.

GUIDONS,—The first, or King's guidon, to be of crimson silk, with a silver and green fringe; in the centre, the rose and thistle conjoined, and crown over them, with the motto, "*Dieu et mon Droit*," underneath; the white horse in a compartment in the first and fourth corners, and XI. D., in silver characters, on a buff ground, in the second and third corners: the second and third guidons to be of buff silk; in the centre XI. D., in silver characters, on a crimson ground, within a wreath of roses and thistles on the same stalk; the white horse on a red ground in the first and fourth compartments, and the rose and thistle conjoined, upon a red ground, in the second and third compartments: the third guidon to have a figure 3, on a circular red ground, underneath the wreath.

General Lord Mark Kerr, after commanding 1752
the regiment twenty years, died in London on

1752 the 3rd of February, 1752; and was succeeded in the colonelcy by his grand-nephew, Colonel William Earl of Ancram, from the Twenty-fourth regiment of Foot.

1755 The United Kingdom was again involved in a foreign war, in consequence of the aggressions of the French on the British territory in North America, in 1755, when the establishment of the ELEVENTH Dragoons was augmented to three hundred and fifty-seven officers and soldiers. A seventh troop was afterwards added, of which Lieutenant William Lindsay was appointed Captain, Cornet John Fletcher Lieutenant, and Charles John Ross, Esq., Cornet, by commissions dated in December, 1755. The seventh troop was mounted on light horses, equipped as light dra-
1756 goons, and designated the *light troop*. Captain Lindsay proved a meritorious and zealous officer; he paid great attention to the mounting, equipping, and training of his troop; and its appearance, with the superior style with which it went through all the evolutions of light cavalry, is commended in the journals of this period.

1757 In the summer of 1757, the ELEVENTH Dragoons were encamped, with five other cavalry regiments, on Salisbury-plain, under Lieut.-General Hawley; and on the 28th of April, 1758, the regiment was reviewed on Datchet-common by King George II., who expressed his

royal approbation of its appearance and disci- 1758
pline.

In the summer of 1758, the light troop was formed in brigade, with the light troops of the First and Third Dragoon Guards, and First, Second, Third, Sixth, Seventh, and Tenth Dragoons, under Brigadier-General Eliott, (afterwards Lord Heathfield,) and employed in an expedition, under Charles Duke of Marlborough, against the coast of France. A landing was effected in Brittany; the troops advanced to *St. Maloes*, and destroyed by fire the magazines, naval stores, and shipping in the harbour. The Light Dragoons particularly distinguished themselves in this service: and the expedition afterwards returned to England. The Duke of Marlborough then proceeded to Germany, and Lieut.-General Bligh took the command of the troops on board the fleet, which proceeded on a second enterprise. A landing was effected in the Bay des Marées; *Cherbourg* was captured; and the fortifications, with the vessels in the harbour, were destroyed, and the brass cannon sent to England. Embarking from Cherbourg, the troops proceeded to the Bay of St. Lunar, and a second landing was effected on the coast of Brittany; the light cavalry again distinguished themselves; but no advantage resulted: and, as the troops were re-embarking, the French attacked the rear-guard,

1758 and the grenadiers of the army, with the First Foot Guards, sustained a serious loss. On the return of the expedition to England, the troops of light dragoons landed and went into cantonments in villages near the coast.

1759 The war in Germany was continued, and the Eleventh Dragoons, commanded by the veteran Lieut.-Colonel William Gardner, whose name appears among the officers at the formation of the regiment in 1715, were selected to proceed on foreign service. Leaving the light troop on coast duty in England, the six heavy troops
1760 embarked in the beginning of April, 1760, landed at Bremen, in Lower Saxony, in the middle of that month, and joined the army commanded by Prince Ferdinand of Brunswick, at Fritzlar, in the principality of Lower Hesse. The Eleventh were formed in brigade with the Scots Greys, under the orders of Major-General Eliott,—the afterwards celebrated defender of Gibraltar.

Towards the end of June the regiment was encamped at Kalle; at the same time thirty thousand French, commanded by the Chevalier de Muy, were manœuvring to cut off the communication of the allies with Westphalia. The regiment left Kalle during the night of the 30th of June, passed the Dymel, and was in position at five o'clock on the following morning, on the heights of Corbeke, from whence it advanced to

the verge of a wood, five miles from the enemy's 1760
position at *Warbourg*. The French were attacked by two divisions of the allied army, and at a critical moment the British cavalry received orders to advance. Traversing the five miles of rugged ground with astonishing celerity, the gallant horsemen arrived at the field of battle at a favourable moment for a charge of the cavalry, and instantly forming, they dashed upon the opposing ranks with the most heroic bravery, overpowered all opposition, and the French were driven across the river Dymel with a heavy loss. Prince Ferdinand of Brunswick was a spectator of the distinguished behaviour of the regiment, and declared in orders, "ALL THE BRITISH CAVALRY PERFORMED PRODIGIES OF VALOUR."

The ELEVENTH having formed and charged the moment they arrived in the field of battle, they were not exposed to the fire of artillery or musketry above five minutes, and their loss was consequently limited to seven horses killed, and a few men and horses injured with bayonet and sabre wounds; one serjeant and two private soldiers, being too eager in the pursuit, were made prisoners.

After this success, the regiment was encamped for some time near Warbourg, and the weather being severe, the soldiers were ordered, on the 10th of October, to build huts for them-

1760 selves, and also for their horses; in December the regiment marched into village cantonments.

1761 Leaving their quarters early in February, 1761, the ELEVENTH Dragoons advanced during a heavy snow into the enemy's cantonments, and the whole army being put in motion, several fortified towns and extensive magazines were captured. After returning from this enterprise, the regiment reposed in cantonments until the beginning of May, when it took the field, and was brigaded with the Second and Seventh Dragoons, commanded by Colonel Edward Harvey of the Sixth. Several weeks were passed in manœuvring and skirmishing; long marches were performed through marshy grounds; days and nights were passed in the open fields, exposed to heavy rains, and in July the regiment was encamped between the Asse and Lippe rivers, forming part of the Marquis of Granby's corps, which had its right in front of the village of *Kirch-Denkern.* When the enemy attacked this post on the 15th and 16th of July, the ELEVENTH were formed in column to support the infantry; the French were repulsed, and the cavalry galloped forward, but were prevented charging by the nature of the ground.

The ELEVENTH were subsequently employed in defensive operations; in August they passed the Dymel, and took part in forcing the French posts beyond that river. On the 3rd of November they made a forced march to Copperbrugge, on the 4th to Dusen; having taken part in driving a body of French from *Capelnhagen*, they were employed, on the 5th of November, in preventing the march of a division of the enemy along the defile leading from Escherhausen to Eimbec. They were at Wentzen on the 6th and 7th of November, and during the night of the 7th they marched through a heavy snow to *Foorwohle*, where they took part in a sharp skirmish. They were subsequently stationed on the heights between Mackensen and Lithorst, and passed the winter in cantonments in East Friesland. 1761

During the campaign of 1762 the Seventh and ELEVENTH Dragoons were formed in brigade under Colonel Hall. On the 24th of June they were employed in the surprise of the French camp at *Groebenstien*, when the enemy left his tents standing, and fell back in confusion upon Cassel, and one of his divisions was surrounded, and made prisoners in the woods of Wilhelmsthal. 1762

In the subsequent part of the campaign, the ELEVENTH were engaged in forcing the French to abandon several strong positions, and in covering the siege of *Cassel*. After the capture of this fortress, a cessation of hostilities took place, which was followed by a treaty of peace.

1763 Having received the thanks of the Parliament for their conduct during these campaigns, with the commendations of the Marquis of Granby and Prince Ferdinand of Brunswick, the ELEVENTH left Germany in February, 1763, and marching through Holland to Williamstadt, embarked for England.

Soon after the arrival of the regiment in England, the *light troop* was disbanded, and eight men of each of the six heavy troops were mounted on light horses, and equipped as light
1764 cavalry. In the following year the regiment was ordered to be remounted with long-tailed horses.

1765 After its return from Germany, the regiment
1767 was stationed in England until the spring of 1767, when it marched to Scotland; and in July its colonel succeeded to the dignity of Marquis of Lothian.

1768 The regiment left Scotland in 1768, and returning to England, was stationed in that part
1772 of the United Kingdom until 1772, when it again proceeded to Scotland, where it passed the succeeding twelve months, and was removed to
1773 South Britain in 1773.

1775 General the Marquis of Lothian died at Bath on the 12th of April, 1775, and was succeeded in the colonelcy of the regiment by Major-General James Johnston from the First Irish Horse, now Fourth Dragoon Guards.

In 1778 the regiment was again stationed in 1778
North Britain, but returned to England in the
following year, when the men of the regiment, 1779
equipped as light cavalry, were incorporated in
the Twentieth regiment of Light Dragoons.

In June, 1780, when the riots occasioned by 1780
a bill being brought into Parliament for the
removal of certain restrictions from his Majesty's
Roman Catholic subjects, took place in London,
the ELEVENTH Dragoons were ordered thither.
They were afterwards stationed at Northampton; 1781
in 1781, at Norwich; and in 1782, they were 1782
employed in suppressing tumults at Nottingham.

At the close of the American war, the value 1783
and importance of light cavalry having become
appreciated, the ELEVENTH were constituted a
corps of LIGHT DRAGOONS. The standard height
for men and horses was lowered; a change of
equipment took place; boots and arms of a
lighter description were adopted, and the cocked
hats were replaced by helmets.

In 1784, the colour of the coats was changed from 1784
scarlet to *blue;* the facings remaining buff as before.

Lieut.-General Johnston was removed to the 1785
Scots Greys in February, 1785, and was suc-
ceeded in the colonelcy of the ELEVENTH LIGHT
DRAGOONS by General the Honorable Thomas
Gage from the Seventeenth Light Dragoons.

In 1786 the regiment was stationed at 1786

1786 Hounslow and Windsor, and performed the escort duty for the Royal Family.

1787 General Gage commanded the regiment two years, and died on the 2nd of April, 1787, when King George III. conferred the colonelcy on General the Honourable Sir Joseph Yorke, K.B., from the Fifth Royal Irish Dragoons, who was
1788 elevated to the peerage in 1788, by the title of Lord Dover, Baron of Dover court, in the county
1789 of Kent. In the following year his Lordship was removed to the First regiment of Life Guards, and the colonelcy of the ELEVENTH Light Dragoons was conferred on General Studholme Hodgson from the Seventh Dragoon Guards.

1790 The riots which took place at Nottingham occasioned the regiment to proceed thither in 1790.

1791 In 1791 the head quarters were at Hounslow, and the regiment performed the escort duty.

In the mean time the political state of Europe had undergone a change; a republican party of a most violent character had gained possession of the reins of government in France, and imprisoned their king. Revolutionary principles were also beginning to manifest themselves in England; but the majority of the people remained firmly attached to their Sovereign, and to the institutions of their country; and a number of persons meeting at Birmingham to celebrate the

anniversary of the French revolution, the house 1791
was surrounded and demolished. A dissenting
minister, Doctor Priestley, being suspected of en-
tertaining revolutionary principles, his house was
destroyed, also several meeting-houses belonging
to the dissenters. To suppress these outrages, a
squadron of the ELEVENTH Light Dragoons, commanded by Captain Michell, proceeded by forced
marches to Birmingham, and order was speedily
restored.

In the summer of 1792 the regiment formed 1792
part of the force encamped on Bagshot-heath,
under the Duke of Richmond, to practise the
system of field movements suggested by Major-
General Dundas, and approved by the king.
His Majesty repeatedly witnessed the perform-
ances of the troops, and expressed his high
approbation of their appearance and discipline.
In December an augmentation of ten men per
troop was ordered; and in February 1793 a 1793
further addition was made to the numbers of the
regiment.

The French republicans having added to their
multiplied acts of cruelty and bloodshed the
murder of their king, this outrage was followed by
war between Great Britain and the French re-
public; and on the 25th of April two squadrons
of the ELEVENTH Light Dragoons, commanded
by Major George Michell, embarked at Black-

1793 wall for Ostend, to join the allied army in Flanders: at this period the regiment consisted of nine troops, and a second lieut.-colonel and a second major were added to the establishment.

This year a serjeant and twenty-five private soldiers proceeded to the West Indies under Lieut.-General Sir Charles Grey; and one corporal and ten private soldiers, with a serjeant and five men of the Fifteenth Light Dragoons, accompanied Lord Macartney on the embassy to China.

The two squadrons on foreign service joined the British and Hanoverian forces commanded by His Royal Highness the Duke of York, co-operating with the Austrians and Prussians, and were engaged in covering the attack of the French fortified camp at *Famars,* near Valenciennes, on the 23rd of May. The enemy was forced from his post, but held a strong redoubt behind Famars until night, when it was evacuated. On the following morning the French, having passed the Scheldt, were seen marching towards Denain; and Captain Charles Craufurd, aide-de-camp to the Duke of York, observing a column of baggage proceeding towards the river, galloped to the ELEVENTH Light Dragoons, who were in advance, and suggested to the commanding officer a sudden attack of the two squadrons. The enterprise appeared hazardous; the French baggage-guard was more numerous than the two squadrons of the ELEVENTH, and was in rear of their own works; the hazard of being cut off was therefore great; yet with that noble daring for which British horsemen have always been conspicuous, the ELEVENTH instantly dashed forward, Captain Craufurd taking the lead, and encouraging the dragoons by his example. Overtaking the enemy's baggage-guard, the ELEVENTH rushed upon them sword in hand with terrific violence, broke them in an instant, sabred fifty men on the spot, took fifty-six prisoners, and captured eight waggons laden with baggage, and thirty horses. A strong body of the enemy advanced to cut off these daring British troopers; but the ELEVENTH effected their retreat with the loss of three men and three horses. His Royal Highness the Duke of York expressed his approbation of the gallant conduct of the ELEVENTH Light Dragoons on this occasion, and commended the behaviour of the officers and men in his public despatch. 1793

The ELEVENTH Light Dragoons formed part of the covering army during the siege of *Valenciennes*, which fortress surrendered to the Duke of York on the 28th of July.

When the siege of *Dunkirk* was resolved upon, the ELEVENTH marched to the vicinity of that fortress, and formed part of the covering

1793 army; but the arrival of the heavy artillery and of the naval force which was to co-operate with the army, was so long delayed, that the French had time to assemble an immense army to raise the siege, which their superior numbers enabled them to effect.

After quitting the vicinity of Dunkirk, the ELEVENTH were engaged in several operations; and in December, when they proceeded into winter quarters, His Royal Highness the Duke of York expressed in orders the high sense he entertained of the intrepidity, patience, and perseverance of the troops, and his confidence that they would prove equally conspicuous for regularity in cantonments, as they had for gallantry in the field.

1794 During the winter the ELEVENTH were employed in piquets and patrole duties between the opposing armies; in February, 1794, they were at Vichte and other villages along the front. In April the allied army was assembled near Cateau, under the Emperor of Austria. On the 17th of April the ELEVENTH supported the attack on the enemy's posts at Vaux, *Prémont*, Marets, and Catillon; they also formed part of the army under the Duke of York, which covered the operations towards Cambray, during the siege of *Landrécies*.

General Otto, having been despatched by the

Duke of York, on the 23rd of April, to reconnoitre 1794 the French force assembling at *Villers en Couchè,* reported them strongly posted, and requested a reinforcement; when several corps, including the ELEVENTH Light Dragoons, were detached for this service. The French were attacked on the following day, and driven into Cambray, with the loss of twelve hundred men, and three pieces of cannon. The ELEVENTH had one man killed on this occasion.

Before daylight on the morning of the 26th of April the British camp on the heights of *Cateau* was alarmed by the report of pistols from the advanced-posts, and soon afterwards the light troops were driven from the villages in front of the army. A thick fog concealed the enemy's movements for some time, but at length the sun broke through, and a body of cavalry was detached to turn their left flank. The cavalry of the left wing also moved forward to reconnoitre the enemy's column which was seen moving from Prêmont and Marets. The Seventh and ELEVENTH Light Dragoons, with two squadrons of Austrian Hussars, being in front, charged and overthrew the enemy's column, and following up their first advantage with the most heroic gallantry, gained a decisive victory over very superior numbers. The brave troopers used their broad swords with such energy and effect, that twelve hundred

1794 Frenchmen lay on the field; and ten pieces of cannon, with eleven tumbrils filled with ammunition, were the trophies of this display of British valour. The impetuosity of the charge was so irresistible, that the French were instantly broken, and the only loss sustained by the ELEVENTH was five horses killed and two wounded. The Duke of York complimented the cavalry on their distinguished conduct, and particularly mentioned the determined gallantry with which the Seventh and ELEVENTH Light Dragoons charged the superior numbers of the enemy on the left.

On the fall of Landrécies, the British removed to the vicinity of *Tournay*, where they were attacked on the 10th of May, and a favorable opportunity presenting itself for turning the enemy's right flank, sixteen squadrons of British and two of Austrian cavalry were detached on this service under Lieut.-General Harcourt, the ELEVENTH Light Dragoons forming part of this force. Having turned the enemy's flank, formidable lines of opponents, six deep, presented themselves, and although the British cavalry charged with their accustomed energy, their first onset was resisted; at the second charge the republican legions were broken, and the British dragoons, dashing fiercely among their discomfited antagonists, spread terror and dismay through the opposing army. Three thousand Frenchmen fell beneath the conquering sabres of the dragoons, four hundred were made prisoners, and thirteen guns remained in possession of the victors. The conduct of the British dragoons was commended by the Duke of York; their loss was not great: the ELEVENTH had seven men and nine horses killed; three men and eight horses wounded. 1794

The ELEVENTH Light Dragoons were engaged in the combined attack made on the French army on the 17th of May, when the British succeeded in performing the part allotted to them; but the Austrian divisions failed, which enabled the enemy to direct so numerous a body of troops against the Duke of York, that His Royal Highness was obliged to retire. The ELEVENTH only lost on this occasion one man, and one horse killed; one quartermaster, one rank and file, and two horses wounded.

Resuming their position near Tournay, the British continued to confront the enemy, until the defeat and retrograde movements of the Austrians rendered a retreat indispensible. Having withdrawn from before Tournay, the British took up several positions to check the progress of the enemy; but it soon became necessary to evacuate the Austrian Netherlands.

In the beginning of January, 1795, the 1795

1795 ELEVENTH Light Dragoons were in position behind the river Waal, which formed a barrier to the advance of the very superior numbers of the enemy ; but the frost was so severe, that a French division was enabled to pass the river on the ice near Bommel on the 4th of January, and on the following day attacked the British troops under Lieut.-General David Dundas at *Geldermalsen*, where the ELEVENTH Dragoons were stationed. After some severe fighting, the enemy was repulsed; the regiment had one man and one horse killed; six men and one horse wounded.

The frost having converted the whole country into a plain, it was found impossible to oppose effectual resistance to the very superior numbers of the French, whose democratical proceedings and doctrines of equality met with a favourable reception from the Dutch, and these circumstances greatly facilitated the progress of the enemy. Long marches over ice, exposure to snow-storms, with a scanty supply of food, and subject to the ill-treatment of the Hollanders, with an enemy ten times more numerous than themselves following them, rendered the sufferings of the British troops, in the retreat through Holland, particularly severe; but on arriving in Germany, they went into quarters of refreshment, and soon recovered from the effects of this winter campaign.

After their arrival in Germany, the British troops were not engaged in any further acts of hostility. The infantry returned to England in the spring of 1795, but the cavalry remained in Germany until the autumn. The ELEVENTH were formed in brigade with the Seventh, Fifteenth, and Sixteenth Light Dragoons, under Major-General Lord Cathcart; the British cavalry and horse artillery being commanded by Lieut.-General David Dundas. During the summer the whole were encamped on the plains of Westphalia. In November the camp broke up, and the ELEVENTH marched to Scharnbeck, where they remained about a month, and afterwards embarked on the river Elbe for England. They commenced their voyage, but were forced by severe weather to the port of Gluckstadt, on the Elbe, a town belonging to the King of Denmark, and situated twenty-eight miles from Hamburgh. The fleet was wind-bound with severe frost six weeks, and afterwards put to sea. 1795

Having landed at Gravesend on the 15th of February, 1796, the two squadrons joined the regiment at Guildford; in August following the ELEVENTH, with five other cavalry regiments and a troop of horse artillery, were encamped near Weymouth, under the orders of Lieut.-Gen. David Dundas. 1796

In this year the men's waistcoats were dis-

1796 continued, and leather pantaloons, half-boots, and a white cloth stable dress was adopted.

1797 In 1797 the regiment was stationed at Windsor and Hounslow, and performed the escort duty for his Majesty; in the summer of
1798 1798 it was encamped on Swinley-downs, with nine other regiments, under Lieut-General David Dundas, and marched, in October, to Dorchester and Sherborne.

On the decease of Field Marshal Studholme Hodgson, in the autumn of this year, the colonelcy was conferred on General the Marquis of Lothian, K.T., by commission dated the 23rd of October, 1798.

1799 Holland had continued, in the mean time, under the French yoke, to which it had become subject during the winter of 1794—5; a numerous body of patriots were, however, believed to remain attached to the House of Orange; and in 1799 a combined British and Russian armament was sent thither, under His Royal Highness the Duke of York, to endeavour to effect the emancipation of the Dutch. The Eleventh Light Dragoons, commanded by Lieut.-Colonel J. Walbanck Childers, marched from Canterbury to Ramsgate, where they embarked for Holland, and arriving in the Texel, swam their horses on shore without any accident, and joined the combined British and Russian forces.

An united French and Dutch force opposed 1799
the advance of the British and Russians; and in the attempt made on the 19th of September, to force the enemy's positions, the ELEVENTH Light Dragoons formed part of the division commanded by Lieut.-General Dundas, and supported the attack on the villages of *Walmenhuysen* and *Schoreldam*. Considerable advantage was gained, but the hasty valour of the Russians led to disasterous results, and the troops fell back to their former positions.

On the 2nd of October another attack was made on the enemy's positions between Bergen and *Egmont-op-Zee*, on which occasion a squadron of the ELEVENTH Light Dragoons, commanded by Captain James Wallace Sleigh, attached to the division under Lieut.-General Dundas, had an opportunity of distinguishing itself. It formed, with a battalion of Russians, the advance of the army, supported by the Fifty-fifth Foot, and fording a deep water, turned the flank of a breastwork, while the Russians stormed the post in front, and the enemy was driven from his works with the loss of two guns. The other columns also succeeded, the cavalry formed in brigade, and advanced along the beach, and the enemy was forced from his posts with great loss. The Duke of York expressed in orders to the troops "his warmest thanks for the

1799 "steady and persevering gallantry of their conduct in the general action of the 2nd instant, "to which alone is to be ascribed the complete "victory gained over the enemy under circum-"stances of the greatest difficulty." The regiment had one man and two horses killed; four men and four horses wounded.

The enemy's posts at *Beverwyck* and Wyck-op-Zee were attacked on the 6th of October, on which occasion two squadrons of the regiment, commanded by Major Henry John Cumming, had their post on the right of a body of Russians, and the other two squadrons under Captain James Wallace Sleigh on the left, in front of Beverwyck. The action was continued with sanguinary obstinacy until night, when the enemy retreated, leaving the British and Russians masters of the field; and His Royal Highness expressed in orders, his "approbation of the "conduct of the two squadrons of the ELEVENTH "Dragoons, attached to the Russian Infantry." The regiment lost ten men killed, and several wounded.

The Dutch people did not second these gallant efforts for their deliverance; and circumstances having occurred which rendered further operations in Holland unadvisable, the army returned, Captain Sleigh's squadron of the ELEVENTH taking part in covering the movement, and

afterwards embarked for England. The regiment 1799
destroyed one hundred and fifty-two horses on the beach for want of transport, and gave fifteen to the Russians. After landing at Yarmouth, it was quartered at Ipswich.

In 1800, when General Sir Ralph Abercromby 1800
was appointed to the command of the British forces in the Mediterranean, he honoured the ELEVENTH Light Dragoons by a personal application to His Royal Highness the Duke of York for a detachment to serve under his command. Four officers and seventy-five rank and file were accordingly embarked for this service under the orders of Captain-Lieutenant A. Money, and sailed to the Island of Minorca, where they landed. Political changes on the Continent of Europe occasioned the first design of the expedition to be laid aside. Towards the end of August the detachment embarked on board the "Diadem," and sailed with the troops designed for the attack of *Cadiz;* but when the fleet arrived off the port, a pestilential disease was raging in the city, and the attempt was abandoned for fear of contagion.

At this time Egypt was occupied by a French army, which had astonished Europe by its successes in Italy and in Germany; had afterwards triumphed in Egypt, and had become inured to the climate of the country. It had

1800 been styled the "Army of the East" by Bonaparte, and against this celebrated body of veterans the British armament was next directed to proceed. The fleet sailed to Malta, where the troops were landed to refresh themselves after being for some time at sea, and the abundance of fresh provisions, which the island afforded, soon restored and reanimated the men.

Leaving Malta on the 20th of December, after a voyage of nine days, the fleet passed through a narrow channel, and entering a magnificent basin of water surrounded by mountains covered with trees, anchored near the town of Marmorice, in Asiatic Turkey, where horses were procured for the cavalry, which now consisted of the Twelfth and Twenty-Sixth Dragoons, forming a brigade under Brigadier-General Finch, and the detachment of the ELEVENTH, with Hompesch's Hussars attached to the reserve under Major-General (afterwards Sir) John Moore.

1801 After arranging a plan of co-operation with the Turks, the fleet put to sea on the 23rd of February, 1801; on the 1st of March it arrived off Alexandria, the ancient capital of Egypt, and on the 8th a landing was effected in the Bay of Aboukir, under a heavy fire of grape and musketry, and the French cavalry and infantry were driven from the shore with loss.

The ELEVENTH Light Dragoons landed and

took part in the operations of the army which 1801
advanced upon *Alexandria*, and on the 13th of March the French were driven from a position which they had taken to oppose the advance. After this victory, the Arabs brought sheep, goats, fowls, eggs, and every thing which the country afforded, to the camp, and five hundred Turks arrived to co-operate with the British. The French at Alexandria, having been reinforced from the interior, attacked the British on the 21st of March, but were repulsed with loss. The glory thus acquired on the distant shores of Egypt was, however, accompanied by the loss of General SIR RALPH ABERCROMBY, who was wounded on this occasion, and died a few days afterwards. The loss of the ELEVENTH was one horse killed; one trumpeter and two rank and file wounded.

Soon after this victory, the ELEVENTH Light Dragoons traversed the country to *Rosetta*, a place distinguished for the beauty of its environs, being embosomed in a grove of date, sycamore, orange, lemon, pomegranate, and palm-trees; and after the surrender of Fort St. Julian, the British and Turkish troops, assembled at this point, moved up the banks of the Nile, through a country abounding in rice, sugar, wheat, barley, and other necessaries and luxuries of life. The ELEVENTH Dragoons, and a body of Turkish

1801 horse, formed the advance-guard; on the 7th of May the French were driven from El-Aft; they were also forced to abandon their fortified post at *Rahmanie*, and retire through the desert to Cairo. In the skirmishing at Rahmanie, the ELEVENTH had one horse killed; one serjeant, one private, and four horses wounded.

Continuing their march along the banks of the Nile, the troops arrived, on the 8th of June, within a few miles of the celebrated Pyramids, where they halted several days; they subsequently advanced to *Cairo*, and after a short siege, the French surrendered.

This conquest reflected additional lustre on the British arms, and the victorious troops retired down the Nile to *Alexandria*, drove in the French posts, and commenced the siege of this fortress, which was surrendered in the beginning of September. Thus Bonaparte's boasted "*invincible legions*" were forced to evacuate Egypt; and the British troops were rewarded with the thanks of Parliament, and the approbation of their Sovereign, who conferred on the ELEVENTH Light Dragoons, and other corps engaged in this splendid enterprise the honour of bearing a "SPHINX," and the word "EGYPT" on their guidons and appointments. The Grand Seignor, to perpetuate the services rendered to the Ottoman empire, established an order of knight-

hood for the British generals and naval officers 1801
of equal rank; gave gold medals to the regimental officers, and commanded a palace to be built at Constantinople for the residence of the British ambassadors. The following officers of the ELEVENTH Light Dragoons received gold medals:—Captain-Lieutenant A. MONEY, Lieutenants BENJAMIN LUTYENS, RICHARD DIGGENS, and JAMES BOURCHIER.

In the mean time the regiment had been 1802
employed in suppressing tumults in various parts of England. In June, 1802, it was reviewed at York by Lieut.-General Staveley, and brought five hundred and five mounted men into the field. In the following month it marched to Wimbledon, and the treaty of peace having been concluded with France, the establishment was reduced to eight troops of seventy-five private men each. The head-quarters were removed to Hounslow in August, when the regiment took the escort duty, and was reviewed by the King on Ashford-common. In September the detachment returned from Egypt.

His Majesty again reviewed the regiment in 1803
June, 1803, and the following notification was received two days afterwards by the commanding officer, Lieut.-Colonel Thomas:—"His Royal "Highness the Commander-in-Chief has to communicate to the ELEVENTH Dragoons that His

1803 "Majesty was most highly pleased with their "military appearance at the review on Monday, the 20th instant; and His Royal Highness is further pleased to signify his entire "approbation of the good appearance of both "officers and men, and the discipline they are "under."

In the mean time the French Consul, Bonaparte, had prepared, under the pretence of colonial purposes, an immense naval and military power, with which he designed to crush, by one mighty effort, the British people, who opposed his schemes of aggrandizement. The British government augmented the army, and took suitable steps to defeat the designs of Bonaparte; and in July the ELEVENTH Light Dragoons marched to the Sussex coast to repel the enemy, should he venture to land. At the same time, the establishment was augmented to ten
1804 troops of ninety-five private soldiers each. In the following year the regiment was stationed on the coast of Kent.

1805 Bonaparte was elevated by the French nation to the dignity of Emperor; and, having reviewed his army at Boulogne, marched, in 1805, to Germany, to crush the coalition forming against his interests. In November of the same year, eight troops of the ELEVENTH Light Dragoons, commanded by Lieut.-Colonel Tho-

mas, marched to Ramsgate to embark for Hano- 1805
ver, where a body of British troops was assembled, under Lieut.-General Lord Cathcart, to co-operate with the continental powers; but some delay having been occasioned by severe weather, the defeat of the Austrian and Russian armies at Austerlitz established the preponderance of French power in Germany; a treaty was concluded at Vienna, the British troops withdrew from Hanover, and the embarkation of the regiment was countermanded.

In the summer of 1806, the ELEVENTH 1806
Dragoons were stationed at Woodbridge, and brigaded with the Sixth and Seventh, under Major-General Lord Paget.

From Woodbridge, the regiment marched, in 1807
the summer of 1807, to Liverpool, where it embarked for Ireland. After landing at Dublin, it marched to Clonmel, Cork, and Fermoy; in
1808, it formed part of a large camp on the 1808
Curragh of Kildare, under Lieut.-General Sir David Baird; and in the autumn, the head-quarters were again stationed at Clonmel.

The regiment occupied quarters at Dublin in 180
1809; in July, 1810, it embarked for England, 1810
landed at Liverpool, and marched from thence to Weymouth.

Portugal and Spain had, in the mean time, been overrun by the legions of Napoleon, who

1811 had placed his brother Joseph on the throne of Spain. A British army, commanded by the Marquis of Wellington, was in the Peninsula; and in April, 1811, eight troops of the ELEVENTH Light Dragoons, mustering seven hundred and twenty-five officers and soldiers, under the command of Lieut.-Colonel Henry John Cumming, embarked at Plymouth for Portugal; they landed at Lisbon on the 31st of May; and after a short halt to refresh the men and horses, marched for Spanish Estremadura to join the army, which had undertaken the siege of Badajoz.

The regiment crossed the Tagus in boats on the 8th of June, and on the 18th arrived at Elvas, in the province of the Alemtejo, a fortress situate on a rocky hill, not far from the river Guadiana. Meanwhile, two powerful armies,—one from the south, under Marshal Soult, and the other, called the army of Portugal, under Marshal Marmont, had advanced to raise the siege of Badajoz: and the British commander, not having forces to withstand such powerful adversaries, and also continue operations against Badajoz, withdrew from before that fortress, and took up a position on the little river Caya. On the following day, the ELEVENTH were formed in brigade, with the Second Hussars of the King's German legion, under the command of Major-General Long.

Having bivouacked in the woods, between 1811
Elvas and the Guadiana, the regiment sent forward a strong piquet, under Captain Lutyens, which took post on the *Caya*, and a piquet of the Second Hussars of the King's German legion was stationed on the Guadiana. The French made a reconnoissance with their cavalry; the horsemen of the army of the south advanced along the Guadiana, and surprised the piquet of the German Hussars, which escaped to Elvas with difficulty and loss. The piquet of the ELEVENTH was observing a body of French cavalry advancing along its front, and did not know of the surprise of the German Hussars; this last circumstance favoured an attempt to surprise the ELEVENTH, which an enterprising French officer, Colonel L'Allemand, effected, by gaining their rear with a body of dragoons, which Captain Lutyens mistook for a regiment of cavalry of the allied army advancing to his support*. Being thus surprised, the piquet of the ELEVENTH was unable to make effectual resistance. Four men were killed; Lieutenant William Smith, and twenty-one rank and file were wounded; Captain Benjamin Lutyens, Lieutenant Thomas Binny, and seventy-five non-commissioned officers and private soldiers, were made prisoners.

* Lord Wellington's despatch.

1811 The opposing armies confronted each other, and the enemy, having a great superiority of numbers, a crisis appeared to be approaching. To dissipate the storm in his front, the British commander induced the Spanish general, Blake, to move down the right bank of the Guadiana, and recross that river at Mertola, with the view of attacking Seville. This movement, apparently so easy, was executed so tardily, that Marshal Soult had time to break up from the Guadiana with part of his army, and reach Seville before the Spaniards. Soult being gone, Marmont prepared to retire; and the English general saw the great body of troops in his front broken up.

Relieved from the presence of two powerful armies, and an intercepted despatch giving reason to believe that Ciudad Rodrigo was in want of provision, Lord Wellington left Lieut.-General Hill with a strong division in the Alemtejo, and marched towards Ciudad Rodrigo, in hopes of surprising that fortress in a starving state; but it was supplied with provision a few days before he arrived on the Coa. The ELEVENTH Dragoons were selected to accompany the main army, and were removed from Major-General Long's brigade, and formed in brigade with the First Hussars, of the King's German legion, under Major-General Victor Alten; on which occasion Major-General Long issued a brigade order, from which the following is an extract:—

"The Major-General would not do justice to 1811
"his feelings, if he refrained from expressing the "very great regret with which he observed, in "the general orders of the 19th instant, the "intended separation of the Eleventh Dragoons "from the brigade under his command. He "begs to assure the officers, non-commissioned "officers, and privates of that corps, that in no "hands could he feel his credit in the field more "securely placed than in theirs; and he is not "less persuaded, by personal observation, than "by the zeal and attention of the officers, and "the orderly behaviour of the men, that their "conduct in quarters would have been equally a "source of gratification to him. The Major-"General requests Colonel Cumming, and the "several officers of the Eleventh Dragoons, "will accept his thanks for their attention and "support: his acknowledgments are not less "due to the non-commissioned officers and pri-"vates, for their steady, creditable, and soldier-"like behaviour during the time they have been "placed under his orders. He wishes sincerely "to the regiment, the attainment of every suc-"cess and degree of glory that valour and disci-"pline can command."

The allied army broke up from the Caya on the 21st of July; on the 22nd the Eleventh commenced their march northward; they crossed

1811 the Tagus by a bridge of boats, at Villa Velha, on the 1st of August, and continued their route upon Ciudad Rodrigo several days; arriving on the confines of Spain, they furnished outposts for the army as usual.

Marshal Marmont had retired from Badajoz to the valley of the Tagus; and being desirous of communicating with General Dorsenne, who had invaded Gallicia, but had been stopped by the arrival of the British on the Agueda, sent forward twelve hundred cavalry and infantry through the mountains which separate Castille from Estremadura. This detachment surprised a piquet of ten men of the ELEVENTH Dragoons, under Lieutenant Frederick Wood, at *St. Martin de Trebejo*, on the 15th of August, and made the whole prisoners.

The regiment advanced to the banks of the Agueda, and took part in the outpost duty on that frontier; two squadrons being at El Bodon, one at Gallegos, and one at Ituera, and *Ciudad Rodrigo* was blockaded. On the 26th of August, the piquet at *Pastores*, about three miles from that fortress, was attacked by a detachment of the enemy, and the ELEVENTH had one man and four horses killed.

Ciudad Rodrigo, having been blockaded six weeks, wanted provision, and on the approach of Marshal Marmont and General Dorsenne, with overpowering numbers, the British commander 1811 established his troops in positions near that fortress; the third division, and two squadrons of the ELEVENTH Dragoons, and one of German Hussars, being stationed on the heights of *El Bodon* and Pastores, on the left of the Agueda, and commanding a complete prospect round Ciudad Rodrigo. On the 24th of September, the enemy introduced a convoy of provisions into that fortress; and at daybreak, on the 25th, fourteen squadrons of the imperial guards drove back the outposts of the left wing of the allied army, but were eventually repulsed. While this skirmish was taking place, thirty squadrons of French cavalry, fourteen battalions of infantry, and twelve guns, advanced towards Fuente Guinaldo. Lord Wellington sent for a brigade of the fourth division from Guinaldo, and afterwards for that part of the third division which was at the village of El Bodon; and, in the mean time, directed Major-General the Honourable Charles Colville to form the Fifth and Seventy-seventh British, and Twenty-first Portuguese, regiments, with a brigade of Portuguese artillery, on the hill over which the road to Guinaldo passed, supporting their flanks with the two squadrons of the ELEVENTH, under Lieut.-Colonel Cumming, and the squadron of German Hussars.

1811 The French squadrons came sweeping over the plain in gallant style; the Portuguese guns smote them with shot; but they passed the front of a ravine by half squadrons, and neither the fire of infantry nor artillery could prevent them ascending the hill. As they pressed forward in heavy masses, the heads of columns were charged and driven back by the two squadrons of the ELEVENTH Dragoons and the squadron of German Hussars. Again, the French horsemen, confident from their superior numbers, (ten to one,) rushed up the hill; and again they were charged, and their leading squadrons broken, and forced back by the gallant British troopers. The French, resolute to win, renewed the attempt to gain the summit of the hill; but were unable to overcome the determined bravery of the few heroic dragoons, who opposed their advance with such astonishing efforts of valour, and charge succeeded charge for upwards of an hour*. Captains MICHAEL CHILDERS and

* "The Portuguese guns sent their shot among Mont- "brun's horsemen in the plain, but the latter passed the front "of the ravine in half squadrons; and neither the fire of "infantry nor artillery could stop them; but they were "checked by the fine fighting of *the cavalry, who charged* "*the head of the ascending masses, not once, but twenty times,* "and always with a good will, thus maintaining the upper "ground above an hour. *It was astonishing to see so few* "*troopers bearing up against that surging multitude.*"— "COLONEL NAPIER'S *History of the Peninsular War.*

CRANSTOWN GEORGE RIDOUT commanded the two squadrons of the ELEVENTH, and highly distinguished themselves. Captain CHILDERS evinced the most heroic gallantry; and, by his example, stimulated his men to feats of valour, which reflected lustre on the regiment to which they belonged. All behaved well; yet Quartermaster HALL was conspicuous for the prowess and daring he displayed, in combat with the crowds of opponents which opposed the two squadrons. 1811

At length the enemy brought up his artillery; and, his squadrons, gaining ground in the centre, captured the Portuguese guns; and one squadron of the ELEVENTH, charging too far, got entangled in the intricacy of the ravine. The Fifth Foot charged and retook the guns; the Seventy-seventh, supported by the Twenty-first Portuguese, repulsed the enemy on the left; but the numbers were too unequal, and the French infantry coming forward, the enemy threatened to envelop and swallow up the few British and Portuguese on the hill; and Lord Wellington ordered the troops to retire from so unequal a contest. The Fifth and Seventy-seventh formed one square, the Twenty-first Portuguese another, and the small body of cavalry and artillery supported the squares; but the French horsemen rushing forward, the British dragoons galloped

1811 to the support of the Portuguese regiment. The two British battalions repulsed a charge of the French squadrons on three faces of their square in a very gallant manner, and afterwards resumed the retreat. Lieut.-General Picton arrived with the troops of his division from El Bodon; and the retrograde movement was continued about six miles, to the entrenched camp at Guinaldo; the enemy following at a distance, and keeping up a sharp cannonade. The loss of the ELEVENTH Dragoons on this memorable day, was one serjeant-major, one serjeant, eight rank and file, and nine horses, killed; Lieut.-Colonel Cumming, Lieut. Charles King, one quartermaster, one serjeant, seventeen rank and file, and twenty-six horses, wounded; Captain Ridout, Lieutenant William Smith, and Quartermaster Hall, had horses killed under them.

In his public despatch, Lord Wellington expressed his "admiration of the conduct of the troops engaged," on this occasion; their behaviour was also held up in general orders as an example to the whole army; and, after narrating the circumstances under which the troops were engaged, it was added, "The commander of the "forces has been particular in stating the details "of this action in the general orders; as, in his "opinion, it affords a memorable example of "what can be effected by steadiness, discipline,

"and confidence. It is impossible that any 1811
"troops can be exposed at any time to the attack "of numbers, relatively greater than those which "attacked the troops under Major-General Col-"ville and Major-General Alten, on the 25th of "September; and the commander of the forces "recommends the conduct of these troops to the "particular attention of the officers and soldiers "of the army, as an example to be followed in "all such circumstances." In these orders the behaviour of Lieut.-Colonel Cumming, of the ELEVENTH Dragoons, was particularly noticed.

The troops afterwards fell back to other positions; and some manœuvring and skirmishing took place, which ended in the retreat of the French, and the advance of the British; the brigade, of which the ELEVENTH Dragoons formed part, taking post at Gallegos, and furnishing the piquets on the left flank of the army. In October, it was relieved from the out-post duty, and marched into winter quarters in Spanish Estremadura, occupying the small, but ancient, town of Coria on the river Alagon; from whence Lieut.-Colonel Cumming proceeded to England, for the benefit of his health; and the command of the ELEVENTH Dragoons devolved upon Lieut.-Colonel James Wallace Sleigh.

From Coria, the regiment was removed in December to St. Miguel; and in January, 1812,

1812 to Chamusca, on the left bank of the Tagus, in Portuguese Estremadura, where it was stationed during the siege and capture of Ciudad Rodrigo.

At this period, the uniform was altered to a coatee, with wide buff facings and silver epaulettes; pantaloons, short boots, and cloth overalls; hussar saddle and blanket; blue horse-furniture, with a border of silver lace; and the helmet was replaced by a chaco.

The British commander having resolved to besiege *Badajoz* once more, the ELEVENTH Dragoons marched to Spanish Estremadura, to form part of the covering army; they crossed the Guadiana at Juramenha, and arrived at Valverde, a small town situate in a pleasant valley, about twelve miles from Badajoz, from whence they sent forward out-piquets. After the capture of Badajoz on the 6th of April, the army proceeded northwards; and Marshal Marmont, who had penetrated Portugal, withdrew, plundering and destroying the country. The ELEVENTH halted at Ituera, from whence the first, second, and third squadrons were detached a short distance to the rear for forage, leaving the fourth squadron at the head-quarters of the army to take the piquets on the Agueda.

In the early part of June, the regiment proceeded to Gallegos, from whence it advanced with the army, and crossed the Agueda, on the

11th of that month; at the same time Colonel 1812
Cumming joined, with a remount of three officers and sixty men and horses from England. Arriving at the vicinity of *Salamanca* on the 16th of June, the ELEVENTH were engaged in driving back the French out-posts, and had two horses killed. On the following day, the army passed the Tormes by the deep fords of Santa Marta and Los Cantos; the French fell back; and as the British marched into position on the mountain of San Christoval, the inhabitants of Salamanca illuminated their houses, and testified their joy by every possible means.

The forts at Salamanca were besieged, and on the 20th of June, Marshal Marmont advanced to their relief, when the British out-posts fell back; some skirmishing occurred, and two men and six horses of the ELEVENTH Dragoons were killed. The French took post behind the villages of Moresco and Castellanos; and on the 22nd, they extended their left, and seized a part of the height in advance of the right wing of the allied army; but they were dislodged by a division under Lieut.-General Graham; the first squadron of the ELEVENTH Dragoons being on the right of the position, took part in this affair, and had one man and four horses killed; two men and seven horses wounded. At night the French withdrew to a position on some heights, about six miles in

1812 the rear; but again advanced; and on the 24th of June they passed the Tormes, and the ELEVENTH Dragoons was one of the corps sent forward to watch their movements. When the enemy saw the order of battle of the allied army, he withdrew; and the forts having surrendered on the 27th of June, he fell back behind the Douro; the British, following by easy marches, overtook the French rear-guard at Rueda, and drove it upon the main body, which was filing across the bridge of Tordesillas. The ELEVENTH were in advance on this occasion, but did not sustain any loss.

In the beginning of July the ELEVENTH Dragoons were formed in brigade with the Twelfth and Sixteenth, under Major-General George Anson.

The French army, being reinforced, passed the Douro on the 15th and 16th of July; and the British commander united his centre and left on the Guarena, but caused the right wing, consisting of two divisions, and Major-General Anson's brigade of cavalry, to halt at *Castrejon*, on the Trabancos, under Lieut.-General Sir Stapleton Cotton. On the 18th, at daybreak, the enemy appeared in force, and drove in the cavalry piquets; the brigade formed in front of the infantry, and afterwards advanced towards the river. Some sharp skirmishing occurred and

the troops maintained their ground until Lord 1812
Wellington arrived, who directed them to retire behind the Guarena. The ELEVENTH had four men and eight horses killed; Lieutenants John Pitt Bontein, and William Williams, six private soldiers, and twenty-six horses wounded; Lieut. Williams died of his wounds; Captain Thomas Jenkins's charger was killed under him.

The opposing armies manœuvred. The French moved up the Guarena on the 20th of July, crossed that river at Canta la Piedra, and directed their march on Salamanca; a corresponding movement was made by the allies, the ELEVENTH Dragoons forming part of the rear-guard, and some sharp cannonading occurred. On the 21st, the allied army occupied his former position on Mount San Christoval, the ELEVENTH being posted, as before, at the village of Moresco; the enemy passed the Tormes, and the British also crossed that river in the evening.

On the 22nd of July, as the French army was manœuvring near *Salamanca*, to gain the road to Ciudad Rodrigo, it was suddenly attacked by the allies, while in the act of performing a difficult evolution, and was routed and driven from the field with severe loss, and its commander, Marshal Marmont, was dangerously wounded. The ELEVENTH Dragoons took part in this glorious achievement, but did not sustain any loss; their

1812 bearing, however, was such as to elicit the commendations of the commander of the forces, and they were rewarded with the royal authority to bear on their appointments the word "SALAMANCA," in commemoration of this splendid triumph over the enemies of their country.*

The darkness of the night favoured the escape of the wreck of the French army; and at daybreak on the following morning the allies advanced in pursuit; the ELEVENTH Dragoons, with the other regiments of their brigade, and two regiments of German cavalry, under Major-General Bock, taking the lead: they were accompanied by the Earl of Wellington, who was soon afterwards rewarded with the dignity of Marquis.

As the two brigades moved up the Tormes, they overtook a strong rear-guard of French cavalry and infantry at a small stream at the foot of a height, near the village of *La Serna*, and instantly charged. The French horsemen fled before the English dragoons, abandoning their infantry, who were broken by the German troopers, and three

* The royal authority for the Eleventh Hussars to bear the word "Salamanca" was granted on the 26th July, 1838, on the application of Lieutenant-Colonel the Earl of Cardigan to the General Commanding-in-Chief, it appearing, on reference to official records, that the Commanding Officer, Colonel Henry John Cumming, had received a medal for being engaged at the battle of Salamanca on the 22nd July, 1812.

battalions were made prisoners of war. The 1812
ELEVENTH had two men and three horses killed on this occasion.

Major-General Anson's brigade continued in advance, and following the rear of the French army, arrived, on the 29th of July, at the banks of the Douro, crossed that river on the following day, and on the 31st entered the ancient city of Valladolid, situate on the banks of the Esquera, in Leon; the French evacuating the place without resistance, and leaving behind them a train of artillery, with ammunition and other stores. The ELEVENTH Dragoons took post on the heights near the town.

When the Marquis of Wellington advanced to Madrid, which was a hundred miles from Valladolid, the ELEVENTH were left, with their brigade and Major-General Clinton's division, on the Douro; the head-quarters of the brigade were at Tudela, a small town on the Douro, five miles from Valladolid, and the ELEVENTH were above thirty miles distant, at Penafiel. When the allied army was gone, General Clauzel advanced with the remains of the army defeated at Salamanca; and on the 13th of August, the regiment was recalled to Tudela. The French regained possession of Valladolid, where twenty thousand infantry, two thousand cavalry, and fifty guns had arrived on the 18th of August. The only British troops to oppose this army, was

1812 Major-General Anson's brigade of cavalry and one division of infantry, and they held their ground as long as possible. On the 18th of August, a body of French from Valladolid drove in the cavalry piquets; an attempt was made to defend *Tudela*, which occasioned the town to be burnt, and the brigade was obliged to pass the Douro. A piquet of the ELEVENTH, under Lieutenant John Peter Lindsell, opposed the advance of the enemy across the bridge with great gallantry, and the Lieutenant, with two men and two horses, were killed. The brigade subsequently occupied villages on the left bank of the Douro.

On the return of the army from Madrid, the troops once more passed the Douro; and on the 6th of September, the first squadron of the ELEVENTH Dragoons, commanded by Lieut.-Colonel Sleigh, with Captains Thomas Jenkins and Peter Augustus Latour, being in advance, surprised and made prisoners the French piquets at *Cisteringa*, in front of Valladolid. Lieut.-General Picton saw the advance of the squadron from an eminence, and declared it was one of the quickest exploits he had witnessed cavalry perform. The squadron had one man killed; and two men and six horses wounded.

The French left their camp, and retired into Valladolid on the same day; during the night they withdrew from the town, and having crossed

the Pisuerga, blew up the bridge. The British 1812
pursued up the beautiful valleys of the Pisuerga and Arlanzan, which were carefully cultivated and filled to repletion with corn, wine, and oil. The ground was favourable for a retiring army, and the French general repeatedly offered battle in strong positions, which were turned by flank movements, when he fell back to other ground, occasional skirmishes taking place. At *Torquemada,* in the beautiful valley of the Arlanzan, a sharp rencounter took place on the morning of the 13th of September, between the piquets of the brigade and a body of French, who were driven across the river. A piquet of the ELEVENTH, under Lieutenant Price, posted on the opposite side of the river, was attacked by three times its own numbers in an open plain, and, although without support, it stood its ground, and beat back the enemy in gallant style: its loss was four men and five horses killed and wounded.

Arriving at *Burgos,* the capital of Old Castille, a place of great antiquity, situate on the declivity, and at the foot of a hill on the right bank of the Arlanzan, the British general undertook the siege of the castle, the ELEVENTH taking part in the outpost duty, and the piquets advancing sixteen miles to *Monasterie.*

A strong reserve of provisional battalions, which Bonaparte had caused to be assembled

1812 and exercised in the Pyrenees, joined the French army, and the command was conferred on General Souham, who advanced to relieve the castle of Burgos. The regiment had previously lost two men and horses, taken prisoners on the outposts; and on the 13th of October a piquet commanded by Captain Latour, was attacked by a body of French, who were driven back with loss, the piquet capturing a number of men and twenty-six horses; the loss of the ELEVENTH was only four horses killed. At length the superior numbers of the enemy obliged the outposts to fall back; and this circumstance, in connection with the movements of two other French armies,—one under Joseph Bonaparte, and the other under Marshal Soult, occasioned the British commander to raise the siege, and retire during the night of the 21st of October; Major-General Anson's brigade taking part in covering the rear. The French pursued; some skirmishing occurred on the 23rd of October; and as a body of the enemy approached *Cellada del Camino*, Major Archibald Money, of the ELEVENTH Dragoons, galloped out from the left of the village at the head of two squadrons, and overturned the leading horsemen of the French army; but the enemy's numbers obliged the two squadrons of the ELEVENTH to fall back on the regiment. Two lines of opponents approached, and the regiment charged and drove the first on

the second, but both coming forward, it was 1812
obliged to withdraw. After some sharp fighting, the army continued its retreat. The regiment lost fifteen men, and nineteen horses killed; Captain William Frederick Schrieber, Lieutenants George Frederick Knipe, and Benjamin Leigh Lye, three serjeants, twenty-three rank and file, and fourteen horses wounded; nine rank and file, and six horses captured by the enemy.

The army fell back to Salamanca, and afterwards to Ciudad Rodrigo, the enemy following, and the ELEVENTH lost several men and horses during the retrograde movement. Arriving on the confines of Spain, they passed the frontier, and went into village cantonments.

On the removal of the Marquis of Lothian 1813
to the Scots Greys, in January, 1813, the colonelcy was conferred on Lieut.-General Lord William Cavendish Bentinck, K.B., from the Twentieth Light Dragoons.

The regiment having sustained, from various causes, a loss of above four hundred men and five hundred horses, was directed to transfer its remaining horses to other corps, and to return to England.

Their removal from the theatre of war was a source of deep regret to the officers, non-commissioned officers and soldiers, who were anxious for additional opportunities to give proof of their innate bravery and zeal for the honour of their

1813 king and country. Their departure also appears, from the following letters, to have been a subject of regret to the major-general commanding the brigade, and to the lieut.-general commanding the cavalry:—

"Sir, "*Aveira, March* 18, 1813.

"It is with extreme regret and concern, "I find, by the general orders of the 13th "instant, that the ELEVENTH Dragoons are "ordered for England; and I cannot withhold "the tribute of praise so justly due to this ex-"cellent regiment, and entreat of you to have "the goodness to communicate to the officers, "non-commissioned officers, and privates, my "very best thanks for their exemplary behaviour "and meritorious conduct since I have had the "honour of having them in the brigade under "my command.

"G. ANSON,
"*Major-General.*

"*To Colonel Cumming,*
"*Commanding Eleventh Dragoons.*"

"Dear Sir, "*Lisbon, June* 2, 1813.

"I was much concerned to find, upon my "arrival in this country, that the ELEVENTH "Dragoons were about to embark for England. "I beg to assure you, the officers, non-com-"missioned officers, and dragoons of the "ELEVENTH, that I regret very much losing the "remains of a regiment which has, at all times,

"conducted itself so much to my satisfaction, 1813
"and which I should be particularly gratified by
"having again under my command. I trust the
"regiment is aware that it was ordered home in
"consequence of its having been so much
"reduced; in other respects, I understand the
"ELEVENTH were in the finest order possible,
"and that the horses were given up in the very
"best condition.

"I am, &c.,

"STAPLETON COTTON,

"*Lieut.-General.*

"*To Colonel Cumming,*

"*Commanding Eleventh Dragoons.*"

The regiment embarked from Lisbon on the 4th of June, arrived at Portsmouth on the 17th, and sailed from thence to Cork, whither the depôt troops had previously proceeded. Having received the horses of the Nineteenth Light Dragoons, who had embarked for Canada, dismounted, the regiment marched to Dublin, where it embarked for Liverpool, and marching from thence to Hounslow, took the escort duty.

1814 By this period the circumstances of the war in the Peninsula had materially changed in favour of the allied armies; the plan of operations of Field Marshal the Duke of Wellington had been attended with the most signal success; the French commander had been forced to abandon one

1814 position after another, until he was driven to the frontiers of France; and the *great nation* was invaded by a victorious British, Spanish, and Portuguese army. The allied sovereigns on the continent were also triumphant, and Napoleon was forced to abdicate the throne of France. The Bourbon dynasty was restored; and when Louis XVIII. left his retreat at Hartwell, to ascend the throne of his ancestors, the Eleventh Light Dragoons furnished his Majesty's escort, and formed part of the cavalcade on his public entry into London on the 20th of April, 1814. They also furnished escorts for the Emperor of Russia, King of Prussia, and other distinguished personages who visited England in the summer of this year. In October, the head-quarters were removed to Canterbury, where a communication was received, authorizing the regiment to bear on its guidons and appointments the word "Peninsula," as a mark of royal approbation of its conduct in Portugal and Spain. Captain Michael Childers received the rank of major, for his services on the staff of the army in Spain and France.

1815 In the spring of 1815, Europe was suddenly alarmed by the return of Bonaparte to France; the French army abandoned its sovereign, who fled to the Netherlands, and the reins of government were once more assumed by Napoleon.

War with the usurper was immediately resolved 1815
upon; and on the 30th of March, six troops of the ELEVENTH Dragoons, mustering four hundred and fifty officers and soldiers, commanded by Lieut.-Colonel SLEIGH, embarked at Ramsgate for Flanders, leaving two troops at Canterbury under Major Horsley. Having landed at Ostend in the beginning of April, the regiment marched to Ghent, to receive the King of France on his arrival at that city on the 6th of April, and afterwards advanced up the country to Eynne, near Oudenarde, on the Scheldt, where it was formed in brigade with the Twelfth and Sixteenth Dragoons, commanded by Major-General Sir John O. Vandeleur, K.C.B. This brigade was reviewed by the Duke of Wellington, soon after his arrival from Vienna, to take the command of the army; and again, on the 29th of May, when the whole of the British cavalry and horse artillery were seen by his grace, in the presence of Prince Blucher, the Prince of Orange, and other commanders.

While the regiment was reposing in cantonments among the Flemish peasantry, Bonaparte assembled an immense body of troops, and attacked the advance-posts of the British and Prussian armies. Orders to advance reached the quarters of the ELEVENTH Dragoons at an early hour on the morning of the 16th of June; and, after marching

1815 a distance of forty-five miles, they arrived at *Quatre Bras,* between six and seven o'clock in the evening, in time to witness the termination of the contest by the repulse and retreat of the French troops; the loss of the ELEVENTH was limited to two horses killed. The regiment bivouacked on the field of battle, and the first squadron formed the advance-piquet in front of the farm-house of Quatre Bras.

The Prussians having retrograded, the British commander fell back to keep up the communication; and the cavalry forming on both sides of the Brussels road to cover the movement, withdrew by brigades as the leading squadrons of the French army approached. The first squadron of the ELEVENTH retired, with the main body of the British cavalry, by the Brussels road, and the second and third squadrons, with five other regiments, by the lower road, through the woods and open country, passing the little river Dyle by a deep ford. Some cannonading and skirmishing occurred; and the first squadron of the ELEVENTH, under the command of Captain Schrieber, was sharply engaged with some French cavalry in the streets of *Genappe,* and evinced signal gallantry. Serjeant Widders particularly distinguished himself, and having cut down an officer of the French lancers, brought off his charger. Four private soldiers of the regiment

were killed on this occasion, and Lieutenant 1815
Moore severely wounded. Having gained the position taken up by the allied army in front of the village of *Waterloo*, the ELEVENTH bivouacked in the rear of the left of the line.

About ten o'clock in the morning of the memorable 18th of June, 1815, the French army was seen advancing to give battle, and as its massy divisions approached, they presented an imposing spectacle. The ELEVENTH Dragoons were formed, with their brigade, in support of the left of the line; when Count D'Erlon's corps developed its attack on the left, they advanced to cover the charge of the Royals, Greys, and Inniskilling Dragoons. When these regiments had overthrown the French infantry, they retired through the intervals of Major-General Vandeleur's brigade, which afterwards resumed its station on the left of the line, where the ELEVENTH remained, skirmishing with the enemy, until about five o'clock in the afternoon. In the mean time a fierce and sanguinary battle had raged at other parts of the field: a large portion of the French army had been annihilated; the British had also suffered severely; and a body of Prussians approaching on the left, the brigade was ordered to the extreme right of the line. Bonaparte having made a last desperate effort with his imperial guards, which had been repulsed, the Duke of Wellington

1815 assumed the offensive, and ordered a general charge of the whole line, when the wings threw forward their outward flanks, the infantry of the centre discharged a last volley, and the whole army rushed forward on the enemy. The fourth and sixth cavalry brigades under Major-Generals Sir John Vandeleur and Sir Hussey Vivian had the honour of leading the attack of the right wing; the fourth brigade scouring the open country, and the sixth advancing nearer the Nivelle road; and both brigades attacked the broken columns of the enemy, and completed their route and discomfiture. The fourth brigade charged two batteries of artillery in the pursuit; and after receiving their fire at the muzzles, cut down the artillery-men, and captured the guns. The pursuit was continued; and when the British halted, the Prussians, who were comparatively fresh, took their place, and followed the wreck of the French army during the night. The Eleventh Dragoons passed the night in the field: their loss was Lieutenant Philips, one serjeant, ten rank and file, and seventeen horses killed; Captain J. A. Schrieber, Lieutenants Frederick Wood, Richard Coles, and Robert Milligan, four serjeants, thirty rank and file, and thirty-eight horses wounded; one serjeant, two trumpeters, twenty rank and file, and eighteen horses missing.

Lieutenant-General the Earl of Uxbridge (now Marquis of Anglesey) having been severely wounded towards the close of the action, the command of the cavalry devolved on Major-General Sir John Vandeleur; that of the fourth brigade on Lieut.-Colonel Sleigh of the ELEVENTH Dragoons; and the command of the regiment on Lieutenant-Colonel A. Money. 1815

The regiment was subsequently rewarded for its distinguished conduct on this occasion with the royal authority to bear the word "WATERLOO" on its guidons and appointments; every officer and soldier received a silver medal to be worn on the left breast; also the privilege of reckoning two years' service for that day. The approbation of His Royal Highness the Prince Regent was also communicated in orders, in which it was stated, "No language can do "justice to the sense His Royal Highness enter-"tains of their distinguished merit, which has "even surpassed all former instances." The approbation of His Royal Highness the Duke of York, commanding-in-chief, with the thanks of His Grace the Duke of Wellington, and of both houses of Parliament, were likewise made known to the troops in general orders.

Lieut.-Colonel James Wallace Sleigh was rewarded with the dignity of a Companion of the Order of the Bath, and the Bavarian order of Maximilian Joseph.

1815 Lieutenant-Colonel A. Money was rewarded with the dignity of a Companion of the Bath; and Majors James Bourchier and Michael Childers with the rank of lieutenant-colonels in the army.

The following officers received medals for the battle of Waterloo:—

Lieut.-Colonel.	*Lieutenants.*	*Cornets.*
J. W. Sleigh.	George Sicker.	B. P. Browne.
Major.	Fred. Wood.	George Schrieber.
A. Money,(Lt.Col.)	Wm. Smith.	Humph. Orme.
Captains.	Rd. Cole.	Hen. R. Bullock.
James Bourchier, (Major)	Benj. Leigh Lye.	P. H. James.
	Jas. R. Rotton.	
Benj. Lutyens	James Moore.	*Pay-Master.*
Michael Childers, (Major)	W. H. Stewart.	Daniel Lutyens.
	Robert Milligan.	
J. A. Schrieber.	Benj. des Voeur.	*Adjutant.*
John Jenkins.		George Butcher.
Thomas Binny		

Quarter-Master, John Hall. *Surgeon*, Jas. O'Malley.
Assistant-Surgeon, H. Steele.

On the morning of the 19th of June the regiment advanced in pursuit of the French army, and arrived before the end of the month in the vicinity of Paris. On the morning of the 2nd of July it crossed the Seine on pontoons, and a squadron escorted the Duke of Wellington to St. Cloud: and on the following day the fourth brigade of cavalry and fifty-second regiment took

possession of the bridge of Neuilly. Paris 1815
having capitulated, the ELEVENTH Dragoons, with three regiments of infantry, accompanied the Duke of Wellington into that city on the 7th of July, the British and Prussians taking the Paris duty, and relieving the French guards in military form.

The regiment remained in the vicinity of Paris, and took part in several grand reviews, at which the Emperors of Russia and Austria, the Kings of France and Prussia, with other distinguished personages, were present.

An army of occupation having been appointed to remain in France, the ELEVENTH Dragoons were selected for this duty, and they were joined by a remount from England. On the breaking-up of the army a general order was published, in which the Duke of Wellington returned "thanks to the general officers, and the officers "and troops, for their uniform good conduct;" and added, "in the late short but memorable "campaign, they have given proofs to the world, "that they possess, in an eminent degree, all the "good qualities of soldiers."

The ELEVENTH were formed in brigade with the Thirteenth Dragoons and Fifteenth Hussars, under Major-General Sir Colquhoun Grant.

In the early part of January, 1816, the 1816
regiment marched to the vicinity of Dunkirk,

1816 the head-quarters being established at Wormhout; it was brigaded with the Seventh Hussars, and was joined in May by two troops from England

In the autumn the regiment removed to the vicinity of St. Omer, and was reviewed by the Duke of Wellington, and afterwards by their Royal Highnesses the Dukes of Kent and Cambridge; it afterwards returned to Wormhout.

1817 The regiment was removed to the vicinity of St. Omer in the summer of 1817; and was again reviewed, with the other British troops in France, in October, by the Duke of Wellington; returning after the review to its former quarters.

1818 After several changes of cantonments the ELEVENTH Dragoons were once more assembled in the vicinity of St. Omer, in August, 1818. In September they were removed to the neighbourhood of Valenciennes, and quartered at Thiant*, and reviewed on the 10th of that month, with the British, Saxon, and Danish contingents, by their Royal Highnesses the Duke and Duchess of Kent.

On the 23rd of October, the Russian, British, Danish, Saxon, and Hanoverian contingents of the army of occupation, went through all the

* An old farmer at Thiant remembered a detachment of the regiment being quartered at his house in 1793, and mentioned the circumstance.

operations of an engagement, in the presence of 1818
the Emperor of Russia, King of Prussia, Prince of Orange, Grand Dukes Constantine and Michael, and other distinguished personages. The army of occupation left France soon afterwards, and the ELEVENTH Dragoons landed, on the 20th and 21st of November [illegible]ver and Ramsgate, from whence they ma[illegible]anterbury.

Immediately on its arrival from France, the regiment received orders to proceed to India: its numbers were fixed at seven hundred and one non-commissioned officers and soldiers, including a recruiting troop, to be stationed at Maidstone; two lieutenant-colonels were also placed on the establishment, and its horses were transferred to other regiments.

On the 7th of February, 1819, five hundred 1819
and forty officers and soldiers of the ELEVENTH Dragoons, commanded by Lieutenant-Colonel Sleigh, embarked at Gravesend, on board the "Atlas" and "Streatham" Indiamen, and arrived on the 1st of July off Sangor Island, where they were removed on board of small vessels, and sailed for Calcutta, at which place they arrived with the loss of four men: three having died on the passage, and one fell overboard, and was drowned.

The regiment was reviewed on the 20th of

1819 July, by General the Marquis of Hastings, who expressed his approbation of its appearance, and made known the excellent character of the corps which he had received from Europe. On the 27th of July and 2nd of August, the regiment embarked in boats, and sailed up the Ganges in two divisions, under Lieutenant-Colonels Sleigh and Childers: it landed at Cawnpore on the 22nd and 27th of October, and received the horses which had belonged to the Twenty-first Light Dragoons, also two hundred men, volunteers from that corps. Twenty-five men of the ELEVENTH Light Dragoons died on the passage up the Ganges.

Major-General Sir Dyson Marshall, K.C.B., inspected the regiment on the 25th of November, and expressed, in the strongest terms, his approbation of its appearance, steadiness, and correct manœuvring. The same sentiments were also expressed by Major-General Sir Gabriel Martindell, K.C.B., at the inspection
1820 on the 3rd of May, 1820; and likewise at the inspection in October following. The regiment suffered much from disease: its loss up to the 1st of September was Lieutenant Gordon, Surgeon O'Malley, Pay-Master Nolan, and one hundred and sixty-six non-commissioned officers and soldiers.

From Cawnpore the regiment commenced its

march in November, by Futty-Ghur, and Ghur-Mockteser, up the right bank of the Ganges, to Meerut, where it arrived on the 6th of December. 1820

At the half-yearly inspections, in April and October, 1821, Major-General Hardyman expressed his approbation in the strongest terms, declaring in orders, that "*he had never before* "*inspected a corps which approached so close* "*to military perfection*;" and his report was followed by a communication from the commander-in-chief, General the Marquis of Hastings, expressing the satisfaction it afforded him on learning the excellent state of the regiment, adding, "The highly gratifying circumstance of "but one court-martial having been considered "necessary in the regiment since the previous "inspection, fully proves the care and attention "bestowed on its interior economy and discipline, and offers the best criterion of the "ability of Colonel Sleigh for command, and of "the zeal and exertions of the officers under him "towards the prevention of crime." The commanding-officer made known to the regiment the estimation in which it was held, with a view to stimulate every individual to support its good character, that the ELEVENTH Light Dragoons might prove themselves a worthy example for other corps to follow. The loss of the regiment 1821

1821 from disease this year was limited to Captain Binny and twenty-eight soldiers.

1822 The reputation thus acquired by the ELEVENTH Dragoons in the distant clime of India, was preserved during the succeeding years; and at
1823 the inspections in 1822, 1823, 1824, and 1825,
1824 orders were issued by the inspecting generals
1825 expressing the very great satisfaction they experienced at witnessing the excellent condition and efficiency of the regiment.

In the mean time, the death of the Rajah of *Bhurtpore* had been followed by an insurruction in his dominions, and his nephew Doorjan-Saul had gained possession of the capital, and placed himself on the throne, to the exclusion of the rajah's son Bulwunt-Singh, who was under the protection of the British authorities. During these proceedings, an army was assembled at Muttra, and the ELEVENTH Dragoons proceeded thither in 1825; but after encamping abo[ut a] fortnight on the banks of the Jumna, they returned to Meerut, and preparations were afterwards made, on an extensive scale, for replacing the rajah on his throne.

In November, an army assembled at Muttra and Agra; the ELEVENTH Dragoons joined the forces at Muttra; their commanding-officer Colonel Sleigh was appointed to the command of the cavalry, with the rank of brigadier-general;

and Lieutenant-Colonel Childers commanded a 1825
brigade, consisting of the ELEVENTH Dragoons and three regiments of native cavalry. The army, commanded by General Viscount Combermere appeared before *Bhurtpore*, the capital, a fortress of immense strength, on the 10th of December, and the siege was commenced with vigour, the cavalry furnishing working parties in the trenches. Several skirmishes occurred between the Bhurtporean horse and the British dragoons; and the cavalry of the besieging army also shared in the toils as well as the danger of the operations. When ground was broke against the fort, a hundred men of the ELEVENTH Dragoons, under Lieutenant Tuckett and Cornet
Bambrick were employed; and in January, 1826, 1826
when a practicable breach was made, Captain Browne, Lieutenant Windus, Cornet Pearson, five serjeants, four corporals, one trumpeter, and eighty private soldiers, volunteered to take part in storming the works, and were placed under the orders of Major Smith of the regiment; but on the arrival of the company's second European regiment, the cavalry volunteers were not required. Bhurtpore was captured by storm on the 18th of January; the castle surrendered, and the usurper Doorjan-Saul, with his wife and two sons, attempting to escape with one hundred and fifty chosen horsemen, were intercepted by

1826 the cavalry under Brigadier-General Sleigh, and made prisoners. The capture of this fortress, with its extensive magazines, annihilated the military power of the Bhurtpore state; the other fortresses submitted, and the youthful rajah was reinstated in his authority. The loss of the ELEVENTH Light Dragoons in this enterprise was two men, and four horses killed; Lieutenant Wymer, twelve rank and file, and twenty-two horses wounded.

On the breaking-up of the army, the regiment was thanked in cavalry orders for its excellent conduct: it marched direct to Cawnpore, where it arrived on the 12th of March, the Sixteenth Lancers having been appointed to take its place at Meerut.

In December the following communication was forwarded to the regiment:—

" *Horse-Guards, 19th Dec.*, 1826.

" My Lord,

" I have the honour to acquaint your lord-
" ship, by direction of His Royal Highness the
" commander-in-chief, that His Majesty has been
" pleased to approve of the ELEVENTH regiment
" of Light Dragoons bearing on its standards
" and appointments, in addition to any other
" badges or devices which may have been hereto-
" fore granted to the regiment, the word
" 'BHURTPORE,' in commemoration of its ser-

"vices at the siege and capture of the fortified 1826
"town and citadel of Bhurtpore, in the month
"of January, 1826.

"I have, &c.,

"Henry Torrens,

"Adjutant-General

General Lord William Bentinck, G.C.B.,
or Officer commanding Eleventh Light Dragoons

The honour of Companion of the Bath was conferred on Colonel Childers.

Preserving their high state of discipline and efficiency, the Eleventh Light Dragoons were thanked in orders at the inspections in 1826, and the subsequent years.

1827 In November, 1827, when General Viscount Combermere reviewed the regiment, he expressed his approbation of its appearance and discipline.

1830 In 1830, orders were issued for the regiment to resume wearing scarlet clothing.

1832 The regiment remained at Cawnpore until the early part of the year 1832; when it commenced its march for Meerut, where it arrived in February, and was stationed at that place during the four succeeding years.

1836 In March, 1836, Lieutenant-Colonel Lord Brudenell, now the Earl of Cardigan, was appointed to the regiment, in succession to Lieutenant-Colonel Michael Childers.

1837 From Meerut the regiment commenced its march, on the 28th of January, 1837, for Cawnpore: it was reviewed on the 31st in camp at Jhautpore, a few miles from Meerut, by General Sir Henry Fane, commander-in-chief in India, who expressed his "perfect approbation of the "soldierlike appearance of the regiment, and of "the fine condition of the horses," which was communicated in orders on the same day; afterwards continuing its route, it arrived at Cawnpore on the 1st of March.

On the 10th of September, Lieutenant-Colonel Lord Brudenell joined at Cawnpore. On the 23rd of October, Lieutenant-Colonel Brutton, after forty-three years' service, retired, resigning the command to his lordship, and took leave of the regiment in orders, in which he declared he could not "find words adequate to express his "sense of the obligation to the officers and men "for the support he has invariably received from "them, in the performance of his responsible "duties; and it is a source of pride and satis-"faction for him to know, that he leaves "unsullied the high character the Eleventh "has ever maintained by their exemplary con-"duct in the field and in quarters."

On the next morning the following orders were issued:—

"Lieutenant-Colonel Lord Brudenell cannot

"refrain from giving expression to the strong 1837
"feelings of pride and satisfaction with which
"he assumes the command of the ELEVENTH
"Light Dragoons,—a regiment whose distin-
"guished services in the field have only been
"equalled by its exemplary conduct in quarters
"on all occasions,—circumstances which are
"both well known to the whole army.

"The Lieutenant-Colonel begs to assure the
"gallant corps he has the honour to command,
"that he is fully sensible of all its merits; and
"he feels confident that by their zeal and co-
"operation, both the officers and non-commis-
"sioned officers will afford him that support
"which, by enabling him to maintain its order,
"discipline, and efficiency, will conduce to the
"welfare and credit of the distinguished regiment
"to which they all belong."

The officers determined to present to Lieut.-Colonel Brutton a piece of plate, as a mark of their regard and esteem for the uniform kindness they had experienced from him, during the period he had commanded the ELEVENTH Light Dragoons. This was communicated to him by Lord Brudenell; and in reply the Lieutenant-Colonel stated,—"I shall proudly accept and "value their kind present, and keep it in remem-"brance of the happy years I have passed in "their society; and when I am no more, leave it

1837 "to my daughter, as a proud testimony of the "esteem in which her father was held in such a "distinguished corps as the ELEVENTH Dragoons. "I beg, my Lord, to return thanks for the hand-"some terms in which you have conveyed to me "the sentiments of my brother officers, as well "as for the personal expressions of regard with "which you have honoured me."

Orders having been received for the ELEVENTH to be relieved by the Third Light Dragoons, and to return to England, one hundred and fifty-eight men volunteered to remain in India,—one hundred and ten in the Third Light Dragoons, and forty-eight in the Sixteenth Lancers; six hundred and nine horses were delivered to the commissariat in high condition; and on the 4th and 11th of December the regiment embarked in two divisions, and sailed down the Ganges to Calcutta.

1838 The first division, under Major Jenkins, arrived at Calcutta on the 15th of January, 1838, and, on the 18th, embarked on board the ship "Thames." The second arrived on the 23rd, and encamped on the glacis of Fort William, remaining there under the command of Lieutenant-Colonel the Earl of Cardigan, who had just returned from leave of absence in the Upper Provinces, until the 2nd of February, when it embarked on board the "Repulse," under Major

Rotton, the Lieutenant-Colonel proceeding to England, *vid* Egypt. 1838

The regiment arrived on the 8th and 25th of June at Gravesend, both divisions disembarking there under the direction of Lieutenant-Colonel the Earl of Cardigan, from whence it proceeded to Canterbury; it brought home three hundred and forty-four non-commissioned officers and soldiers, of which number one hundred and twenty were invalided.

On the 6th of August the regiment was formed into six troops; its establishment being three hundred and thirty-three non-commissioned officers and soldiers.

In 1839, Indian saddle pannels were intro- 1839
duced into the regiment instead of horse blankets, which were discontinued. Holsters were laid aside, and a supply of new accoutrements was received; the regiment was also furnished with new Victoria percussion carbines.

On the 11th of June the regiment was inspected by Major-General Sleigh, inspecting general of cavalry, and the following regimental orders was issued on the occasion:—

"The inspection of the regiment having been "this day completed, the Lieutenant-Colonel has "much pleasure in notifying to the troops, that "Major-General Sleigh has assured him of his "approbation of their appearance in the field, as

1839 "well as of that of every department in barracks; and has informed the commanding "officer, that he will request the General Commanding-in-chief to review the regiment.

"In making this intimation, the Lieutenant-"Colonel begs leave to express his own satisfaction at the progress which has been made in "the re-organization of the corps since its return "from India: he begs to offer his thanks to "the officers and non-commissioned officers, "for their steady attention to their respective "duties, and for the support and assistance "which they have thereby afforded him in establishing a system of duties, to many of which "the greater portion of the troops were entirely "unaccustomed, after so long an absence in a "distant climate.

"The Lieutenant-Colonel feels confident, that "but one feeling prevails in the corps, viz., a "desire to uphold its honour and credit, and to "maintain that high character which it has ever "borne in the army.

"The Lieutenant-Colonel has great satisfaction in making this announcement to the "regiment on the anniversary of the arrival of "the first division of it in Canterbury barracks, "on their return from India."

His Royal Highness the Duke of Cambridge reviewed the regiment at Canterbury, on the

21st of June, and expressed to Lieut.-Colonel 1839 the Earl of Cardigan, "in the strongest terms, "his approbation of the appearance and steadi-"ness of the troops in the field and on parade, "and of the progress which has been made "towards the efficiency of the regiment." The same sentiments were also expressed by Lieut.-General Sir Hussey (late Lord) Vivian, when he reviewed the regiment on the 28th of June.

On the 22nd of June, Lieutenant-General Lord Charles Somerset Manners, K.C.B., was appointed colonel of the regiment, in succession to General Lord William Bentinck, deceased. Lord C. S. Manners reviewed the regiment on the 16th of July, and expressed the high sense he entertained of the honour of being appointed colonel of so distinguished a corps.

General Lord Hill, commanding-in-chief, reviewed the ELEVENTH Light Dragoons, on the 6th of August, at Canterbury, and made known, in the strongest terms, his approbation of the rapid progress the regiment had made towards efficiency, since its return from India. Field Marshal the Duke of Wellington saw the regiment on the 16th of October, and expressed the same sentiments.

The following Regimental Order was issued on this occasion:—

"The Lieutenant-Colonel feels the greatest

1839 "pleasure in communicating to the regiment "which he has the honour to command, that "Field-Marshal the Duke of Wellington has "expressed his high approbation of the rapid "completion of the efficiency of the regiment in "so short a space of time since its return from "the East Indies.

"His Grace was also pleased to refer with "satisfaction to the services of 'his old friends "the ELEVENTH Light Dragoons in the Penin- "sula.'

"The Lieutenant-Colonel requests that the "officers and non-commissioned officers will "accept his thanks for their exertions in carrying "into effect the various duties of the regiment. "He also begs to express his satisfaction at the "creditable manner in which the troops paraded "this day for the review, as also for their steadi- "ness in the field.

"The Lieutenant-Colonel feels confident that "all ranks must be highly gratified at the honour "of being reviewed by that illustrious General "Field-Marshal the Duke of Wellington."

Lieutenant-General Lord Charles Somerset Manners was removed, on the 8th of November, to the Third, or the King's own Light Dragoons, and was succeeded by Major-General Philip Philpot.

1840 On the 7th of February, 1840, the regiment

furnished escorts to attend His Royal Highness PRINCE ALBERT OF SAXE-COBOURG, from Dover to Canterbury, on his way to London; the prince having arrived in this country for the purpose of being married to Her Majesty QUEEN VICTORIA. On the following morning, a squadron escorted His Royal Highness from Canterbury, the first stage on the road to London. 1840

The following letter was received on the 14th of March, conveying Her Majesty's most gracious pleasure for the regiment to be appointed Hussars, and to be styled THE ELEVENTH, OR PRINCE ALBERT'S OWN HUSSARS.

"*Horse-Guards, March* 12, 1840.

"My Lord,

"I have the honour to acquaint you, by "direction of the General Commanding-in-chief, "that Her Majesty has been graciously pleased "to direct that the ELEVENTH Regiment of Light "Dragoons shall be armed, clothed, and equipped "as Hussars, and styled the 'ELEVENTH, OR "PRINCE ALBERT'S OWN HUSSARS.'

"I have, &c.,

"J. MACDONALD, Adjutant-General.

"*Lieut.-Col. the Earl of Cardigan,*
"*Commanding Eleventh, or Prince*
Albert's own Hussars."

1840 In consequence of this communication the clothing was changed from a chaco, scarlet jacket, and blue overalls, to a fur cap, blue jacket and pelisse, and crimson overalls; and the shabracque from blue to crimson.

Major-General Philpot was removed to the Eighth Hussars on the 30th of April, and Her Majesty conferred the colonelcy of the ELEVENTH HUSSARS on HIS ROYAL HIGHNESS FRANCIS ALBERT AUGUSTUS CHARLES EMANUEL, DUKE OF SAXE, PRINCE OF SAXE-COBOURG AND GOTHA, K.G. AND G.C.B.

A notification of the intended removal of the regiment to Brighton having been received, the inhabitants of the city of Canterbury presented the following address, through the corporation, expressing their regret at the departure of the regiment, and their approval of its uniform good conduct on all occasions.

"*To the Right Honourable the Earl of Cardigan,*
"*Lieutenant-Colonel of the* ELEVENTH
"*(Prince Albert's Own) Hussars.*

"My Lord,

"We, the undersigned citizens and inhabit-"ants of the city of Canterbury, hear with "extreme regret that your stay in these quarters "is limited to a few days, and we lose not a "moment in tendering to your Lordship and the

"regiment an earnest expression of our esteem 1840
"and regard.

"Having had an opportunity for a considerable time past of estimating from personal knowledge the noble, courteous, and gentlemanly bearing of your Lordship and the officers under your command, as well also of the meritorious and respectful deportment of the men, we trust confidently that your Lordship will not consider us presumptuous in requesting your acceptance of this humble tribute of our feelings.

"Deeply do we regret your departure from our ancient city; indelibly will the gratifying recollection of your residence here be impressed upon our minds. The best wishes of the citizens will follow you to your future quarters, where we are fully assured, that the greater the facilities afforded you of displaying your noble and generous qualities, the more highly will they be appreciated and admired.

"Confident that the laurel will ever adorn the crown of Great Britain whilst her army retains its present perfect discipline, we take our leave of the ELEVENTH Hussars with an earnest prayer for, and fervent interest in, their future welfare and honour."

In reply to the address, Lieutenant-Colonel the Earl of Cardigan stated,—"I beg you will

1840 "assure the citizens and inhabitants of Canterbury, that it affords me the greatest satisfaction "to receive through the hands of the deputation "which I have now the pleasure to address, the "very flattering testimony of their approbation, "which you have done me the honour to communicate from them.

"My brother officers, as well as myself, will, "I am convinced, feel highly gratified by this "expression of your good opinion.

"You have been pleased to state that you "regret the departure of the regiment which I "have the honour to command, from your "ancient city; allow me to assure you that we "shall always reflect, with feelings of the highest "satisfaction, on the recollection of your testimony of esteem and regard.

"It affords me very great satisfaction to "learn, that the respectful deportment of the "men of PRINCE ALBERT'S HUSSARS has been "such as to attract your notice; that by such "good conduct they have given another proof of "their being worthy of those high honours "which have recently been conferred on the "regiment by Her Most Gracious Majesty the "QUEEN, and that they are not unmindful of "that very important duty of living upon terms "of harmony and good fellowship with the "respectable citizens among whom they may be "ordered to be stationed.

"I beg you will accept my most sincere 1840
"wishes, as well as those of my brother officers, "for the welfare and prosperity of the city of "Canterbury."

The regiment marched from Canterbury on the 23rd of June, and relieved the Twelfth Royal Lancers at Brighton and Chichester.

On the 1st of April, 1841, the regiment left 1841
Brighton, and marched to Hounslow and Hampton-Court, and took the QUEEN's duty.

The regiment was inspected on the 3rd and 5th of June by Major-General Sleigh, who expressed his entire "approbation of its appearance in the field, and the quickness and steadiness with which the manœuvres were performed." He was also "much pleased with "the inspection of the regiment in barracks."

Field Marshal His Royal Highness Prince Albert reviewed the ELEVENTH HUSSARS on the 9th of June, and was pleased to express "his "high approbation of the appearance and movements of the regiment."

On the 13th of June, a line of escorts attended the QUEEN from Buckingham Palace to Nuneham, in Oxfordshire, and on Her Majesty's return, on the 15th;—on this occasion the QUEEN was pleased to command the Master of the Horse, the Earl of Albermarle, to communicate to the General Commanding-in-chief,

1841 "Her Majesty's entire approval of the good "order and conduct of the several escorts." The Earl of Albermarle's letter was forwarded to Lieutenant-Colonel the Earl of Cardigan, by the Adjutant-General, who stated that Lord Hill had "derived the greatest satisfaction from the "perusal of that communication," the contents of which he desired the Earl of Cardigan would be pleased to insert in regimental orders. The General Commanding-in-chief also expressed, through the Quarter-Master General, "his entire "satisfaction at the proper and effective manner "in which the service was performed."

The ELEVENTH HUSSARS furnished the escorts which attended the QUEEN to Woolwich, on the 21st of June, on the occasion of the launch of Her Majesty's ship "Trafalgar;" and on the 15th of July, they were reviewed by their Royal Highnesses the Duke and Duchess of Cambridge, who expressed the high gratification they experienced at witnessing the excellent condition of the regiment.

Escorts were furnished by the ELEVENTH HUSSARS, on the 26th of July, to attend the QUEEN from Windsor Castle to Woburn and Pansanger in Bedfordshire; and an escort of the regiment accompanied Her Majesty to the seat of His Grace the Duke of Bedford, remaining in quarters on the road until the Queen's return.

General Lord Hill expressed, through the Quarter-Master General, "great satisfaction at the "judicious arrangements made by Lieutenant-"Colonel the Earl of Cardigan, for carrying his "instructions into effect; and also at the precision "and regularity with which they had been acted "upon by the officers, non-commissioned officers, "and private men." 1841

The ELEVENTH, OR PRINCE ALBERT'S HUSSARS, furnished escorts, on the 22nd of January, 1842, for His Majesty the King of Prussia, from New Cross to Staines, on his way to Windsor Castle; His Majesty having arrived in this country to be present at the christening of the Prince of Wales; and on the 28th of that month, the regiment was reviewed at Windsor, in brigade with the Royal Horse Guards, by Her Majesty the QUEEN, accompanied by the King of Prussia, Prince Albert, the Duke of Wellington, and other distinguished persons. The QUEEN'S royal approbation of the appearance and movements of the regiment, on this occasion, was communicated to the officers and men in regimental orders, also the satisfaction expressed by the King of Prussia, Prince Albert, &c. 1842

On the 4th of February, the ELEVENTH HUSSARS escorted the King of Prussia to Woolwich, where His Majesty reviewed the troops stationed at that place, and embarked immediately afterwards for Ostend.

1842 A relay of escorts attended the QUEEN, on the 10th of February, from Staines to the Royal Pavilion at Brighton; and the General Commanding-in-Chief again expressed "his perfect "satisfaction with all the arrangements made "under the direction of Lieutenant-Colonel the "Earl of Cardigan, and with the manner in "which they had been carried into effect."

On the 20th April the regiment was reviewed by the Queen on Wimbledon-common, on which occasion His Royal Highness Prince Albert marched past at the head of the regiment, and saluted Her Majesty. Field-Marshal the Duke of Wellington was present at this review. Her Majesty was graciously pleased to communicate to Lieutenant-Colonel the Earl of Cardigan her entire approval of the regiment.

On the 25th of April, His Royal Highness Prince Albert was appointed by Her Majesty to the Colonelcy of the Third, or Scots Fusilier Guards, and Lieut.-General Sir Arthur Benjamin Clifton, K.C.B., from the Seventeenth Lancers, was appointed to be Colonel of the ELEVENTH, HUSSARS. Her Majesty was at the same time graciously pleased to command, that the regiment should retain the designation of "THE PRINCE ALBERT'S OWN HUSSARS."

About the end of April, the ELEVENTH HUSSARS were relieved in the royal escort duties

by the Eighth Royal Irish Hussars, and were re- 1842
moved from Hounslow and Hampton-Court to York, Barnsley, and other towns in Lancashire.

On the 30th August Lieutenant-General Charles Murray, Lord Greenock, K.C.B, was appointed to the Colonelcy of the Eleventh Hussars, in succession to Lieutenant-General Sir Arthur Benjamin Clifton, K.C.B., who was removed to the First or Royal Dragoons.

The foregoing pages detail many proofs of the efficiency and gallant conduct of the regiment at home and abroad, and of its having, on all occasions, evinced a soldier-like spirit, and a regard for discipline; qualities which have rendered this excellent corps worthy of possessing the confidence of the crown and kingdom, and of the distinguished honour of bearing the title of the name of the illustrious consort of Her Majesty Queen Victoria.

1842.

SUCCESSION OF COLONELS

OF

THE ELEVENTH,

PRINCE ALBERT'S OWN REGIMENT OF LIGHT DRAGOONS;—

HUSSARS.

PHILIP HONEYWOOD,

Appointed 22nd July, 1715.

PHILIP HONEYWOOD obtained a commission in a regiment of foot in 1694, and served under King William III. in the Netherlands. In the reign of Queen Anne he shared in the toils and dangers of two campaigns in Brabant, under the celebrated John Duke of Marlborough, and afterward transferred his services to Spain, and was rewarded for his excellent conduct with the lieut.-colonelcy of Wade's, now thirty-third, regiment. In 1709 he was promoted to the colonelcy of a newly-raised regiment, and in 1710 he obtained the rank of brigadier-general. He was a zealous and warm-hearted advocate for the Protestant succession, and on the formation of a new ministry, which was believed to be favourable to the interests of the Pretender, he was guilty, together with Lieut.-General Meredith and Major-General Macartney, of drinking, on a public occasion, a toast which was offensive to the government, and they received an official intimation that the Queen had no further occasion for their services. Four years afterwards a change took place; the ministers who had induced the Queen to deprive him of his commission were charged with high treason, and fled to France, and Brigadier-General Honeywood was rewarded for his attachment to the house of Hanover, with a commission to raise, form, and discipline a corps of cavalry, now the ELEVENTH, PRINCE ALBERT'S OWN REGIMENT OF LIGHT DRAGOONS, HUSSARS. He served at the head of his regiment during the rebellion of the Earl of Mar, commanded a brigade at Preston, and was wounded at the storming of one of the avenues of the town, on which occasion he evinced signal valour and judgment. In 1719 he commanded a brigade in the expedition against Spain, under Lieut.-General Lord Cobham; he took possession of the town of Vigo with eight hundred men, and was afterwards engaged in the siege of the citadel, which surrendered in a few days. He was promoted to the rank of major-general in 1726, and in 1727 he was placed on the staff of the army held in readiness to embark for Holland. After commanding the ELEVENTH Dragoons seventeen years, he was removed to the Third Dragoons, and in 1735, he was promoted to the rank of lieut.-general. He commanded the army sent to Flanders in 1742, until the arrival of the Earl of Stair, and in the following year he was promoted to the rank of general, and appointed colonel of the King's Horse, now First Dragoon Guards. At the battle of Dettingen he commanded the cavalry of the front line; he also served in Germany, and was rewarded with the dignity of Knight of the Bath, and the appointment of

Governor of Portsmouth. He died in 1752, and was buried with military honours at Portsmouth.

Lord Mark Kerr,

Appointed 29th May, 1732.

Lord Mark Kerr, son of Robert, fourth Earl and first Marquis of Lothian, chusing the profession of arms, was appointed captain of a company of foot on the 1st of January, 1694; and on the breaking out of the war in the reign of Queen Anne, he obtained the lieut.-colonelcy of General Macartney's newly-raised regiment, (afterwards disbanded,) with which he embarked from Scotland in the spring of 1704, and served the campaign of that year on the Dutch frontiers. In January, 1706, he was promoted to the colonelcy of a newly-raised regiment, and embarked with this corps with the expedition against France under the Earl of Rivers, and when that enterprise was laid aside, he sailed to Spain and joined the troops under the Earl of Galway. He was at the head of his regiment at the battle of Almanza, and was posted between two brigades of Portuguese cavalry, which galloped out of the field at the first attack; his regiment was afterwards fiercely engaged with superior numbers and nearly annihilated. His Lordship was wounded in the arm; his lieut.-colonel and major were both killed, and he had twenty other officers killed, wounded, and taken prisoners. His regiment was subsequently sent to England to recruit; in February, 1711, he was promoted to the rank of brigadier-general, and his regiment served on board the fleet as marines, but was disbanded at the treaty of Utrecht; at the same time

Queen Anne conferred on his Lordship the colonelcy of the Twenty-ninth Foot. He commanded a brigade under Lord Cobham at the capture of Vigo, Rondendella, and Pont-a-Vedra, in 1719; in December, 1725, he was removed to the Thirteenth Foot; and was promoted to the rank of major-general in 1727. In 1732, King George II. gave him the colonelcy of the ELEVENTH Dragoons; promoted him to the rank of lieut.-general in 1735, and conferred on his Lordship the government of Guernsey in 1740. In 1743 he was promoted to the rank of general; he was appointed governor of Edinburgh Castle in 1745, and placed on the staff of Ireland in 1751. He died on the 2nd of February, 1752. It is recorded that, "He "was a man of marked and decided character; with "the strictest notions of honor and good-breeding, he "retained, perhaps, too punctilious an observance of "etiquette, as it gave him an air of frivolity. He was "soldierlike in his appearance; formal in his deport-"ment; whimsical, even finical in his dress; but he "commanded respect wherever he went, for none "dared to laugh at his singularities. Manners, which "in foreign courts (where they had been acquired,) "would have passed unobserved, were considered as "fantastic in his own country, and were apt to lead his "impatient spirit into rencontres too often fatal to "his antagonists. Naturally of a good temper, his "frequent appeals to the sword on trivial occasions "drew on him the imputation of being a quarrelsome "man; but he was inoffensive unless provoked; and "never meddled with any but such as chose to meddle "with him*."

* Douglas's Peerage by Wood.

William Henry Earl of Ancram,

Appointed 8th February, 1752.

William Henry Earl of Ancram, chusing the military profession, was appointed to a commission in the Eleventh Foot in 1735, and in 1741 he was promoted to captain and lieut.-colonel in the First Foot Guards. He acted as aide-de-camp to the Duke of Cumberland at the battle of Fontenoy, where he was severely wounded by a musket ball in the head. In the same year he was promoted to the rank of colonel in the army, and appointed to the lieut.-colonelcy of the Eleventh Dragoons, at the head of which corps he served during the rebellion in 1745 and 1746, and commanded the cavalry of the left wing at the battle of Culloden, where his brother, Lord Robert Kerr, was killed. After this victory he commanded the forces at Aberdeen, and on the east coast of Scotland, where the Eleventh Dragoons were stationed, until August, and in December he again accompanied the Duke of Cumberland to the Netherlands. He was promoted to the colonelcy of the Twenty-fourth Foot in 1747; and in 1752 he succeeded his grand uncle, Lord Mark Kerr, in the Colonelcy of the Eleventh Dragoons. In 1755 he was advanced to the rank of major-general; in 1758, to that of lieut.-general, and in the summer of the last-named year, he commanded a division in the expedition to St. Maloes, under Charles Duke of Marlborough. He was many years a member of Parliament, and succeeded, on the decease of his father in 1767, to the dignity of Marquis of Lothian. In 1768 he was chosen one of the representatives of the Scottish Peerage, and invested with the Order of the

Thistle: in 1770 he was promoted to the rank of general. He died at Bath on the 12th of April, 1775.

JAMES JOHNSTON,

Appointed 26th April, 1775.

JAMES JOHNSTON was many years an officer of the Royal Horse Guards (Blues); he served at the battles of Dettingen and Fontenoy, and was promoted to the majority of the regiment in November, 1750, and to the lieut.-colonelcy in December, 1754. He commanded the Blues at several actions in Germany during the seven years' war, and was rewarded, in 1762, with the colonelcy of the First Irish Horse, now Fourth Dragoon Guards. He was promoted to the rank of major-general in 1770, and was removed to the colonelcy of the ELEVENTH Dragoons in 1775. He was further advanced to the rank of lieut.-general in 1777, and was removed to the Scots Greys in 1785, the colonelcy of which corps he retained until his decease in 1795.

THE HONORABLE THOMAS GAGE,

Appointed 4th February, 1785.

THE HONORABLE THOMAS GAGE, son of Thomas, first Viscount Gage of Castle Island in Ireland, was several years an officer of the Forty-fourth Foot, and was promoted to the lieut.-colonelcy of the regiment on the 26th of February, 1751. He was serving with the Forty-fourth, in North America, when hostilities commenced between the British and French, respecting the boundaries of their possessions, and commanded the advance-guard at the disastrous engagement near Fort du Quesne, on the 9th of July, 1755, and was wounded. During the contest which followed, he was distinguished for zeal, activity, and personal bravery, and in 1758 he was appointed colonel of a corps of provincials which was numbered the Eightieth, or light armed, regiment of foot. He commanded a brigade in North America, and after the conquest of Canada, he was rewarded with the rank of major-general; at the close of the seven years' war his regiment was disbanded, and he was appointed colonel of the Twenty-second Foot. In 1770 he was promoted to the rank of lieut.-general, and in April, 1774, he was appointed captain-general and commander-in-chief of Massachusetts' Bay, and arrived at Boston in the following month. The American war commenced in the succeeding year, and his zeal to force the revolted provincials to return to their obedience, was followed by the appointment of commander-in-chief in North America in August, 1775, which, however, he only held a few months. In 1782 he was removed to the Seventeenth Light Dragoons, and promoted to the rank of general; in 1785 he was removed to the colonelcy of the ELEVENTH Light Dragoons, which he retained until his decease in 1787.

JOSEPH, LORD DOVER, K.B.,

Appointed 4th April, 1787.

JOSEPH YORKE, third son of Philip, first Earl of Hardwicke, entered the army at an early age, and was aide-de-camp to the Duke of Cumberland at the battle of Fontenoy. He was subsequently aide-de-camp to King George II., and in 1755 he was appointed colonel of the Ninth Foot. In 1758 he was removed to the Eighth Dragoons; in 1760 to the Fifth Dragoons; and in 1787 to the ELEVENTH Light Dragoons. In 1788 he was advanced to the Peerage, by the title of LORD DOVER, Baron of Dover Court in the county of Kent; and in the following year he was appointed colonel of the First regiment of Life Guards. He died in 1792.

STUDHOLME HODGSON,

Appointed 13th March, 1789.

STUDHOLME HODGSON, after serving several years in the army, was appointed, in 1745, aide-de-camp to the Duke of Cumberland, whom he attended at the battles of Fontenoy and Culloden. He obtained the command of a company, with the rank of lieut.-colonel, in the First Foot Guards, on the 22nd of February, 1747; and on the 30th of May, 1756, he was promoted to the colonelcy of the Fiftieth Foot. He obtained the rank of major-general on the 25th of June, 1759; and was removed to the colonelcy of the Fifth Foot in October of the same year. In 1761 he was advanced to the rank of lieut.-general, and he commanded the land forces of a successful expedition against Belle Isle in the same year, for which he obtained the approbation of the King, and received the expression of the "warm sense of the great service he "had done his King and country;" also the congratulation, "on the completion of so important and critical "an operation, which must ever be remembered to his "honour," from the Secretary of State, the celebrated

William Pitt, afterwards Earl of Chatham. He was appointed in 1765, governor of Forts George and Augustus. In 1768 he was removed to the King's Own; in 1778 he was promoted to the rank of general; and in 1782 he was removed to the coloneley of the Fourth Irish Horse, now Seventh Dragoon Guards. He was again removed, in 1789, to the ELEVENTH Light Dragoons, and on the 30th of July, 1796, he was promoted to the rank of Field-Marshal. He enjoyed this elevated rank two years, and died in the autumn of 1798, at the advanced age of ninety years.

WILLIAM JOHN MARQUIS OF LOTHIAN, K.T.,

Appointed 23rd October, 1798.

WILLIAM JOHN LORD NEWBATTLE was appointed cornet in the ELEVENTH Dragoons in 1754; in 1759 he was promoted to the majority of the Nineteenth Dragoons, and in 1760 to the lieut.-colonelcy of the Twelfth Dragoons; in 1766 he was removed to the Fourth Irish Horse, now Seventh Dragoon Guards, and in 1767, he obtained the designation of EARL OF ANCRAM. In 1771 he was appointed lieut.-colonel of the Scots troop of Horse Grenadier Guards; and he succeeded to the title of MARQUIS OF LOTHIAN in 1775. The Order of the Thistle was conferred on his Lordship in 1776, and in 1777 the colonelcy of the First troop of Life Guards, which was constituted the First regiment of Life Guards in 1788. During the indisposition of King George III., the Marquis of Lothian voted, on the important question of the regency, for the right of the Prince of Wales, and signed the protest on that subject; and on His Majesty's recovery he was removed from his command. In 1796 his Lordship was promoted to the rank of general; and in 1798 His Majesty gave him the coloneley of the ELEVENTH Light Dragoons, from which he was removed to the Scots Greys in 1813. He died in 1815.

LORD WILLIAM HENRY CAVENDISH BENTINCK.

Appointed 27th January, 1813.

LORD WILLIAM H. C. BENTINCK, second son of William Henry, third Duke of Portland, chusing the profession of arms, was appointed ensign in the Second Foot Guards, in January, 1791. In 1792 he obtained the King's permission to serve as a volunteer with the Prussian army under the Duke of Brunswick, about to enter France, but on arriving on the continent, leave to serve was refused by the Duke. Returning to England, he obtained a captaincy in the Scots Greys, and in 1793 he was removed to the ELEVENTH Dragoons. He accompanied his regiment to Flanders, was appointed aide-de-camp to the Duke of York, and was at the action of Famars, and sieges of Valenciennes and Dunkirk. At the end of the campaign he returned to England, and embarked, as aide-de-camp to lieut.-general the Earl of Moira, with the forces designed to aid the French royalists of La Vendée, who were in arms against the republicans. This expedition was held in suspense during the winter; and in February, 1794, Lord William Bentinck was promoted major of the Twenty-eighth Foot, and in March, lieut.-colonel of the Twenty-fourth Light Dragoons, then first embodied. He served the following campaign with the Duke of York's army in Flanders, and, returning to England during the winter, was appointed aide-de-camp to the King, with the rank of colonel in the Army. In May, 1799, he was appointed by His Majesty to remain at the head-quarters of Marshal Suwarroff's army in Italy, where he continued until the beginning of 1801, and was present at several battles which took place during that period. In July, 1801, he proceeded to Egypt, and returned in January, 1802. In April, 1803, his Lordship sailed for India as governor of Madras, where he displayed a wise and liberal policy, as well as skill on military subjects, and was promoted to the rank of major-general in 1805. In January, 1808, he returned to England, and was appointed in August, to the staff of the army under Lieut.-General Sir H. Burrard, in Portugal; he was afterwards employed on an important mission to the Supreme Junta in Spain. He subsequently joined the army under Lieut.-General Sir John Moore, and at the battle of Corunna he commanded a brigade, (Fourth, Forty-second, and Fiftieth regiments,) which occupied one of the most important points in the position, and highly distinguished itself.

In 1809 Lord William Bentinck again proceeded to Portugal, and held an appointment on the staff of Lord Wellington's army with the local rank of lieut.-general and was, soon afterwards, appointed Minister at the court of Sicily and commander-in-chief of His Britannic Majesty's forces in that island. In 1810 he was appointed colonel of the Twentieth Light Dragoons, and was promoted, in 1811, to the rank of lieut.-general. The line of policy adopted by his

Lordship in Sicily, secured the independence of that island. A Sicilian Parliament was assembled in 1812, and a government having been established in the island, Lord William Bentinck proceeded with a body of troops to Spain, and landed them in Catalonia. In January, 1813, he was removed to the ELEVENTH Light Dragoons. He returned to Sicily in October, 1813, and in 1814, he left that island with a body of troops, and at Leghorn he published a proclamation, inviting the Italians to shake off the French yoke. He subsequently landed his troops, and, after a few slight actions, made himself master of Genoa. At the close of the war he resided some time at Rome. In 1825 he was promoted to the rank of general; he was also rewarded with the dignity of Knight Grand Cross of the Order of the Bath, and Knight Grand Cross of the Royal Hanoverian Guelphic Order; and in 1827 he was appointed Governor-General of India, having been previously sworn a member of the Privy Council. He was nominated commander-in-chief of the army in India in 1833; he returned to England in 1837. He died at Paris, in June, 1839.

LORD CHARLES SOMERSET MANNERS, K.C.B.,
Appointed 22nd June, 1839.

REMOVED to the Third Light Dragoons 8th of November, 1839.

PHILIP PHILPOT,
Appointed 8th November, 1839.

REMOVED to the Eighth Hussars, 30th of April, 1840.

His Royal Highness Francis Albert Augustus Charles Emanuel, Duke of Saxe, Prince of Saxe-Cobourg and Gotha, K.G., G.C.B.,

Appointed 30th April, 1840.

Removed to the Third, or Scots Fusilier Guards, on the 25th of April, 1842.

Sir Arthur Benjamin Clifton, K.C.B., & K.C.H.,

Appointed 25th of April, 1842, *from the 17th Lancers.*

Removed to the First, or Royal, Dragoons, on the 30th August, 1842.

Charles Murray, Lord Greenock, K.C.B.

Appointed 30th August, 1842.

London:
Harrison and Co., Printers,
St. Martin's Lane.

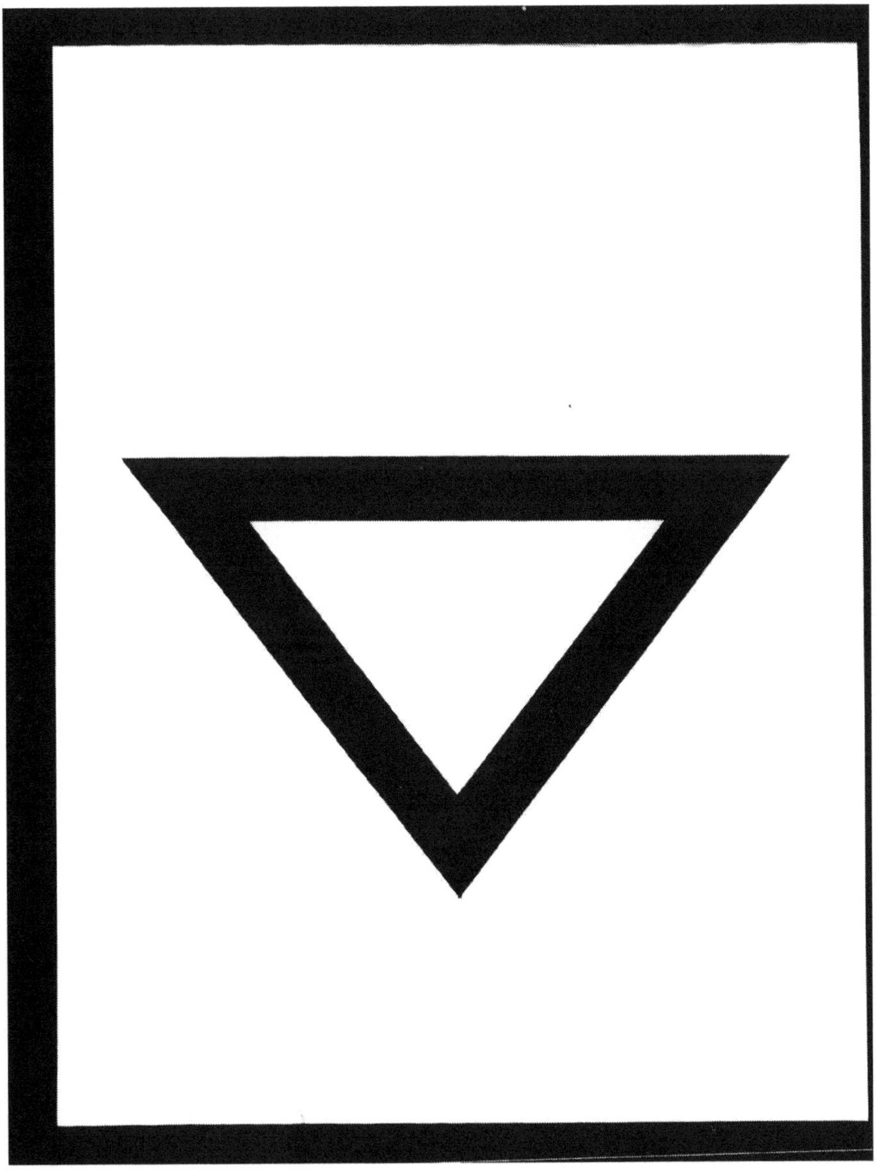

Lightning Source UK Ltd.
Milton Keynes UK
UKHW051031230123
415755UK00013B/75

9 781015 367371